INITIATIC
EROTICISM

N° 2 - 15 Novembre 1930 - Prix : 1 franc

LA FLÈCHE

ORGANE D'ACTION MAGIQUE

La Flèche paraît le 15 de chaque mois. — Prix du numéro : 1 fr. — Abonnement d'un an : 10 fr. — Souscriptions bénévoles pour soutenir le journal : 25 fr. et 50 fr. Ces souscriptions donneront droit à quelques publications spéciales au cours de 1931. — Toute correspondance doit être adressée à la Directrice, Mme MARIA DE NAGLOWSKA, 11, rue Bréa, Paris-6°.

Le Livre de la Vie

Satan, le Fils, la Femme

deux pôles du même axe. Celui qui s'incline devant le Fils s'incline devant son ennemi Satan, et celui qui s'incline devant [...] de la chute, est précipité dans la création ne peut concevoir son salut en dehors du salut des autres. Car les autres sont lui, et il est les autres. *Le Père n'a rien créé sans le Fils* et toutes choses existent par le Fils: ce dogma [...]

La Flèche *No. 2, the rarest of all the issues of* La Flèche

INITIATIC
EROTICISM

AND OTHER
OCCULT WRITINGS
FROM *LA FLÈCHE*

MARIA DE NAGLOWSKA

Translated from the French with an
Introduction and Notes by Donald Traxler

Inner Traditions
Rochester, Vermont • Toronto, Canada

Inner Traditions
One Park Street
Rochester, Vermont 05767
www.InnerTraditions.com

Text stock is SFI certified

Translation, introduction, and commentary © 2013 by Donald C. Traxler

Originally published in French from 1930–1935 as the monthly newspaper
La Flèche: Organe d'Action Magique
Part VI, "Contributions of Julius Evola," is used with permission from the
Fondazione Julius Evola, Rome.

Library of Congress Cataloging-in-Publication Data
Naglowska, Maria de, 1883–1936.
  [La Fleche, organe d'action magique. English]
  Initiatic eroticism and other occult writings from La Flèche / Maria de
Naglowska ; translated from the French with an introduction and notes by
Donald Traxler.
      p. cm.
  Includes bibliographical references and index.
  ISBN 978-1-59477-479-9 (pbk.) — ISBN 978-1-62055-153-0 (e-book)
  1. Occultism. 2. Sex—Miscellanea. 3. Erotica—Miscellanea. I. Traxler,
Donald. II. Title.
  BF1442.S53N3413 2013
  133—dc23
                                                          2013011142

Printed and bound in the United Staes by Lake Book Manufacturing, Inc.
The text stock is SFI certified. The Sustainable Forestry Initiative® program
promotes sustainable forest management.

10 9 8 7 6 5 4 3 2 1

Text design and layout by Priscilla Baker
This book was typeset in Garamond Premier Pro with Democratica, Broadway,
and Gill Sans used as display typefaces

CONTENTS

PART VI

CONTRIBUTIONS OF JULIUS EVOLA TO *LA FLÈCHE*

INTRODUCTION

THE ORGAN OF MAGICAL ACTION

Donald Traxler

If we could go back to the Paris of the early 1930s and stroll the streets of Montparnasse, we might easily meet an attractive Russian woman sitting in a café surrounded by occultists. Or, we might see her selling her little newspaper in front of the café. That woman was Maria de Naglowska, and the little monthly newspaper she was selling, of either eight or sixteen pages depending on her finances at the time, was *La Flèche, Organe d'Action Magique*. In English, *The Arrow, Organ of Magical Action*. If the reader guesses that the title may have been a phallic reference, the reader is correct—and it was intended that way.

Shocking? Probably not so much for that time and place or for that woman who was herself considered shocking by many.

Maria was influential among the Surrealists, and they seem to have influenced her own writing. Naglowska's sessions are said to have been attended by the avant-garde and the notorious of the time, including Man Ray, William Seabrook, Michel Leiris, Georges Bataille, and André Breton. Jean Paulhan, for whom *L'Histoire d'O* was written, is also said to have attended. I have not yet been able to trace these often-made claims to reliable, original sources, so for now, they should be regarded as hearsay. An example of the difficulty of verifying the other names is the claim made for both Bataille and Paulhan in *Demons of the Flesh* by Nikolas and Zeena Schreck.[1] Unfortunately the only supporting reference the Schrecks give for Naglowska is to an earlier article by Nikolas Schreck. Their bibliography does not include anything by Bataille, Paulhan, or Naglowska (although they mentioned Naglowska seventy-four times in their book), and the claim is not supported in any footnote or endnote. It must, therefore, be considered hearsay, at least for now. In the case of William Seabrook, his connections with Man Ray and Michel Leiris are well known and documented by both their and his own writings. Whether Seabrook did indeed attend Naglowska's sessions is not proven as far as I am concerned. I have read his autobiography and the biography written by his second wife, Marjorie Worthington, and found nothing. The only indication that Seabrook was aware of Naglowska, other than his association with Man Ray and other surrealists, is in a Wambly Bald piece in the Paris edition of the *Chicago Tribune* for November 3, 1931. A perhaps telling fact, though, is that both Naglowska and Seabrook studied philosophy at the University of Geneva before the First World War. It is interesting to note that in Marjorie Worthington's biography of Seabrook she states that he considered himself a Catholic (although he was the son of a Protestant minister and had been raised as a Protestant). This self-identification, apparently without external practices, could have been due to Naglowska's influence.

We know that surrealist poet and painter Camille Bryen was a member of Naglowska's group from the short biography titled *La Sophiale* by Marc Pluquet.[2] I have drawn most of the details about Naglowska's life from this biography since it is, by far, the most reliable source. The Bryen connection was also cited in John Patrick Deveney and Franklin Rosemont's *Paschal Beverly Randolph: A Nineteenth-Century Black American Spiritualist.*[3]

The writer Ernest Gengenbach also appears to have been a part of Naglowska's group according to the Foreword in the Deveney and Rosemont book.[4] Rosemont also mentions Gengenbach's connection with Naglowska, further evidenced in one of Gengenbach's own writings. It also seems significant that one of the best studies of Naglowska was done by another surrealist, Sarane Alexandrian, in *Les libérateurs de l'amour.*[5]

Until recently, Maria de Naglowska was almost unknown to the English-speaking world. Those who knew her at all probably knew her as the translator of Paschal Beverly Randolph's *Magia Sexualis,* for which she did far more than translate. Now, a realization is growing that Naglowska was an important religious innovator, an interesting thinker, and a fine writer. The scandalous image is something that she seems to have carefully cultivated for her own purposes.

The present volume, the fifth in a series of Naglowska translations, reinforces what we learned from the earlier ones, and shows another of her facets: that of the journalist. The quality of Maria's writing should not surprise us, because all her adult life she lived by writing. The difference is that unlike the journalism that supported her family, in *La Flèche* and in the other books published in this series the subject matter was spiritual, sexual, and magical.

Who was this strange woman who peddled her newspaper on the streets of Montparnasse?

Maria de Naglowska was born in St. Petersburg in 1883, the daughter of a prominent family. She went to the best schools and got the best education that a young woman of the time could get. She fell in love with a young Jewish musician, Moise Hopenko, and married him against the wishes of her family. The rift with Maria's family caused the young couple to leave Russia for Germany and then Switzerland. After Maria had given birth to three children, her young husband, a Zionist, decided to leave his family and go to Palestine. This made things very difficult for Naglowska, who was forced to take various jobs as a journalist to make ends meet. While she was living in Geneva she also wrote a French grammar for Russian immigrants to Switzerland. Unfortunately, Naglowska's libertarian ideas tended to get her into trouble with governments wherever she went. She spent most of the 1920s in Rome, and at the end of that decade she moved on to Paris.

While in Rome Maria de Naglowska met Julius Evola, a pagan traditionalist who wanted to reinstate the pantheon of ancient Rome. Evola was also an occultist, being a member of the Group of Ur and counting among his associates some of the followers of Giuliano Kremmerz. It is said that Naglowska and Evola were lovers. It is known, at least, that they were associates for a long time. She translated one of his poems into French (the only form in which it has survived), and he translated some of her work into Italian.

While occultists give a great deal of weight to Naglowska's relationship with Evola, it is clear that there must have been other influences. Some believe that she was influenced by the Russian sect of the Khlysti, and some believe that she knew Rasputin (whose biography she translated). Maria, though, gave the credit for some of her unusual ideas to an old Catholic monk whom she met in Rome. Although Maria said that he was quite well known there, he has never been identified.[6]

Maria said that the old monk gave her a piece of cardboard, on which was drawn a triangle, to represent the Trinity. The first two apices of the triangle were clearly labeled to indicate the Father and the Son. The third, left more indistinct, was intended to represent the Holy Spirit. To Maria, the Holy Spirit was feminine. We don't know how much was the monk's teaching and how much was hers, but Maria taught that the Father represented Judaism and reason, while the Son represented Christianity, the heart, and an era whose end was approaching. To Maria, the feminine Spirit represented a new era, sex, and the reconciliation of the light and dark forces in nature.

It is mostly this idea of the reconciliation of the light and dark forces that has gotten Maria into trouble, and caused her to be thought of as a Satanist. Maria herself is partly responsible for this,

Maria de Naglowska

having referred to herself as a "satanic woman" and used the name also in other ways in her writings. Evola, in his book *The Metaphysics of Sex,* mentioned her "deliberate intention to scandalize the reader."[7] Here is what Naglowska herself had to say about it.

> *Nous défendons à nos disciples de s'imaginer Satan (= l'esprit du mal ou l'esprit de la destruction) comme vivant en dehors de nous, car une telle imagination est le propre des idolâtres; mais nous reconnaissons que ce nom est vrai.*
>
> [We forbid our disciples to imagine Satan (= the spirit of evil or the spirit of destruction) as living outside of us, for such imagining is proper to idolaters; but we recognize that this name is true.]

In 1929 Naglowska moved to Paris, where she got the unwelcome news that she would not be given a work permit. Deprived of the ability to be employed in a regular job, she would have to depend on her own very considerable survival skills. She began work on the book for which she is best known today, her "translation" of *Magia Sexualis*,[8] by Paschal Beverly Randolph. This work by the American hermetist and sex theorist is known only in Naglowska's "translation." I have put the word "translation" in quotation marks because it is really a compilation. Less than two-thirds of the work can be identified as being from Randolph. The rest is from sources only beginning to be identified, or from Naglowska herself, and the organization of the material is clearly her contribution as well.

While Naglowska was working on *Magia Sexualis,* she began giving lectures or "conferences" on an original teaching of her own. She called it the "Doctrine of the Third Term of the Trinity." Her conferences were, at first, often held in cafés. The proprietors of these venues were pleased with the influx of patrons and often gave Maria free food and coffee. In a short time her following grew to the point where she could afford to rent a room for private meetings, which, according to Pluquet,[9] usually held thirty to forty people when it was full, and the overflow stood in a "baie vitrée," or glassed-in bay, which separated the hall from the entrance. The hall in question was the old Studio Raspail at 46 Rue Vavin (not to be confused with the present cinema on Bd. Raspail). The building now houses an Italian restaurant that has a capacity of 120 seats. The space may have been enlarged, or it may not. The low divider that formed the "baie vitrée" is still there, but it no longer seems to have glass over it. It would take a sizable crowd to fill the space and still have overflow standing in the entryway. On page 14 Pluquet states that all of these "conferences" were taken down in shorthand by a certain Mr. Dufour. Unfortunately, these shorthand notes have not yet surfaced.

It was thus that Maria survived. Maria's income was supplemented by her publishing endeavors. After the 1931 publication of

Magia Sexualis, Naglowska turned to writing original works. One of these, *Le Rite sacré de l'amour magique,* a metaphysical novelette apparently containing elements of her own life, was published as a supplement to her street newspaper in early 1932, having earlier been serialized in her newspaper.[10] The little newspaper, to which she and other occultists contributed, was the public voice of her magical group, La Confrérie de la Flèche d'Or (Fraternity of the Golden Arrow). The little newspaper would eventually number twenty issues in its five-year existence.

The next of her original works, *La Lumière du sexe,*[11] [The Light of Sex] was published in late 1932. It was the first of two works, the other was *Le Mystère de la pendaison*[12] [The Hanging Mystery] that were required reading for initiation into La Flèche d'Or.[13] These books are now quite rare. To my knowledge, neither they nor any of Naglowska's other original works had ever been translated into English before their translation in this series.

Maria de Naglowska is said to have been very psychic. She predicted the calamity of the second world war,[14] and in 1935 she had a dream presaging her own death.[15] Knowing that she was going to die, she refused to reprint *La Lumière du sexe* and *Le Mystère de la pendaison,* which had both sold out. She told her followers that nothing would be able to be done to spread her teachings for two or three generations.[16] She went to live with her daughter in Zurich, and it was there that she died, at the age of fifty-two, on April 17, 1936.

It is clear to me, having now read virtually all of Naglowska's surviving writings, that she was not a Satanist. She was, on the other hand, a mystic, a philosopher, and a superb writer. I shall be happy if the present translation makes her known and accessible to a wider audience than she has heretofore had. Maria de Naglowska's writings have spoken strongly and with great vitality to me, and it is my belief that they will speak so to many others.

A NOTE ON THE TRANSLATION

Naglowska often expressed herself in symbolic language. Some of this language was evidently intended to shock and to draw attention to herself and her teachings (two things not easily done in the vibrant and decadent Paris of the 1930s). My original plan was to simply translate this symbolic language into English and let it speak for itself. This is, indeed, what I have done in the translation. But I recently read a passage in Pluquet's biography where Maria told her disciples that her teachings "would need to be translated into clear and accessible language for awakened women and men who would not necessarily be symbolists."[17] I knew then that Maria would want more. I have, therefore, included some explanatory expansions on the text in footnotes.

Maria de Naglowska had an aristocratic education, and her French was impeccable. She did not waste words or multiply them unnecessarily. Her writing style is chiseled and classical, worthy of a Voltaire or an Emerson. I have done my best to reproduce her style in these pages.

I have also tried in this translation to transmit Maria de Naglowska's vision, unencumbered by the nonsense that has been written about her by some. Hers is a magnificent vision, with the potential to uplift those who share it.

DONALD TRAXLER began working as a professional translator (Benemann Translation Service, Berlitz Translation Service) in 1963. Later he did translations for several institutions in the financial sector. On his own time he translated poetry and did his first metaphysical translations in the early 1980s. He later combined these interests, embarking on an ambitious, multiyear project to translate the works of Lalla (also known as Lalleshvari, or Lal Ded), a beloved fourteenth-century poet of Kashmir Shaivism. That project is still not complete, but many of the translations have become favorites of contemporary leaders of the sect. He is currently focusing on Western mysticism in a five-book series on Maria de Naglowska for Inner Traditions. He is contemplating a major project on another European mystic and an eventual return to and completion of the Lalla project. Except for Lalla, he translates from Spanish, French, and Italian. All of his projects are labors of love.

PART I

The Book of Life

The Book of Life is the earliest exposition of Naglowska's doctrine of the Third Term of the Trinity, and it thus has great historical importance. It was serialized in La Flèche *from October 15, 1930, through March 15, 1931. The first chapter, "The Trinity and the Triangle," appeared in* La Flèche *No. 1, dated October 15, 1930. It was the lead article on the first page of this first issue, which perhaps indicates the great importance that Naglowska attached to it.*

1

THE TRINITY
AND THE TRIANGLE

The Breath of Life has a three-beat rhythm. This is why the Trinity is holy. First there is the Splendor, which descends, then the Profanation, which moves horizontally, and lastly the Glory, which again climbs.

The Doctors of the Christian church named these Three, respectively: the Father, the Son, the Holy Spirit. They were right, for it was their era, but we say: "the Father, the Son, the Woman." We could also say, although for less delicate ears: "the Descent, the Suffering in the body, the new Ascension."

The error of Christian doctrine was to attribute the whole Work to the Christ: that is to say to the incarnation of just the second term. Yet this error can be explained, because the Woman (the Holy Spirit) cannot do anything without the Son, and the glory cannot be attained without the previous profanation. The glory of the Woman is the glory of the Son and in Her is accomplished His redemption. "When the left shall be as the right," Jesus said.*

---

*[Jesus may have said it, but he did not say it anywhere in canonical literature. A similar saying is found in some Apocryphal documents, such as the Acts of Peter. —*Trans.*]

Our epoch is that of the third term, because the divine Ascension is now beginning, and that is why it is only now that our new dogmas can be clearly announced in the public square. Nothing is comprehensible to the crowds if the hour has not yet sounded. Therefore we render homage to the learned men of the Church for having known how to keep the secret until the end.

The Profanation (the Son) proceeds from the Splendor of the Father (the Fall). This is evident because the rays come from the light and are lost in infinite space. But the Splendor continues until the last stage of the fall and grieves for the children who have lost their way and calls them back. The line is then broken, and it turns. It sees in front of itself the emanation of the first term, the negative of the Father, the luminous points of the descent projected upon the horizontal line of the road of the profanation that has been traveled. This emanation has the vague form of a woman; it is illusion, attraction, the mysterious charm whose promise is not clear. A struggle begins: a voluptuousness. The glory of the Son begins only when the Woman has won, because preciseness of divine memory is necessary to bring about the return of happiness and well-being, and the woman cannot speak while the man is standing.

Naturally, the return does not take place on the horizontal line of sorrows. The return is a new path that will leave a trace where there is as yet none. When the third way has been run, the Triangle will be perfect, and the Three will be One concretely, just as they eternally are in the abstract. It is then that humanity will have its era of complete satisfaction and "all things shall be new" [Revelation 21:5] as promised.

We say, as did the doctors of the earliest Christian church: the Son is born eternally of the Father and the Woman (the Holy Spirit) emanates ceaselessly from the first term. But we add: the Woman is not made manifest except thanks to the defeat of the Son. In this sense she belongs to the Father and to the Son. On this point, we approach Rome while distancing ourselves from Byzantium.

The complete text of our dogma of the Trinity is as follows:

We know that the Trinity is holy. We know that they are Father, Son, and Woman, that Their glory is one and that Their life is eternal.

We know also that humanity is the arena or the projection of the Divine Comedy in three acts: The generation of the Son by the Father, or the fall of the divine into the creation; the profanation of the Father by the Son or the painful affirmation of the Son through created forms; the glorious return of the Son toward the Father, thanks to the attraction of the Spouse, or the work of the divine rebirth.

Human history translates this Divine Comedy thus: first there is the Pyramid (see "Our Social Thesis"),* then its collapse, and finally its rebuilding by new means.

The rebuilding begins today, and the new means are brought by woman, or rather through woman. But we are only in the early hours. We are like a train whose locomotive only has crossed the threshold of the tunnel. The cars are still in darkness, and no one is able to see the new countryside except the travelers in the first compartments.

What they see in the new land is the act of redemption: the woman attracting the man not for his degradation, but to set up again in him the spiritual strength that had been put to sleep in a materialization of fleeting solace.

This cannot be summarized—given the shadows that surround us—more clearly than as follows: the companion of the man in the new land offers the divine energy liberated in her, not for procreation, but to foster in him the vision of the plane of the Splendor. How? It is only possible to know with long preparation, yet the train

---

*[Here Naglowska is referring to another article in the same issue of *La Flèche*. Since it is not part of The Book of Life, it appears in a separate section of this anthology. —*Trans.*]

that we are is advancing, and the number is growing of those who conceive of it naturally.

The hour approaches when everyone will know the secret, and it is then that the selection will be made. For there will be those who succeed and those who do not succeed. That will depend on the interior purity that each brings to the liberating test.

This will be the baptism of the new religion, of the Religion of the Third Term. The respective merit of each person will be manifested infallibly, and the hierarchy that results will be indisputable.

Obviously, those who wish to be the first, those who wish to succeed only to place themselves above the others, will necessarily fail, for pride is a clear proof of non-enlightenment. Pride is there where the spine is not straightened, where the divine does not penetrate because egotism resists. Artificial magic will never obtain the results of natural magic, because only the latter comes from God.

This leads us to say that if it is true that starting now we are entering into the era of liberation, it is no less true that all will not participate in the same measure in the glory of the Son regenerated. The worst will not even be able to pass the opening of the tunnel and will suffocate in the darkness. But their inferiority will not long trouble the celebration of the Groom, for the breath of Life will leave them quickly. There will be weeping and gnashing of teeth, but it will be justice.

The question of divine justice is thorny, and it is even impossible to resolve it by considering it from below, that is to say with care for the welfare of each one. According to us—we insist—human beings do not in themselves present an object of interest, just as for an electrical engineer the question is not one of making all wires good, but of choosing the best for the electrical installation that he proposes. The Son must be reborn, and each one is not necessarily required for that: so much the better for those who are useful to Him, so much the worse for those who are not.

On this point, we completely detach ourselves from the Christian spirit that gives short shrift to supreme values while losing itself in the labyrinth of human miseries, and with joy we greet the modern rebirth of the spirit of generous boldness that lessens vain care for the welfare of each while replacing it with bold scorn of death. It is a good beginning and one that will bear fruit when its spiritualization deepens.

Divine justice is large and vast, but it is not composed only of mercy, of the famous "kindness" imagined by Christians that is a fall and which causes the fall. Mercy is inherent to the Holy Trinity since the Father is a member of it. The second term, the Son, is the sad consequence of Kindness from which comes his revolt along the horizontal line. It is the expiation of the fall, and for that reason the Profanation is a holy work. We will have much to say about it later.

The third term, the Spouse, corrects the rebellious march of the Son by orienting it toward glory. Her hour is sounding today and that is why a change is beginning to take shape in the world. Those humans (the conducting wires) who rigidly remain on the horizontal and do not bend themselves in the direction of the new orientation cease to serve the passage of the Glorious. Because of that, they are destined for degradation, that is to say the descent by stages into the lower kingdoms of life: animals, plants, and minerals. It is at this point, also, that we insert our theory of deposition, which we oppose to Darwinian evolution with all the force of our conviction. But this will be developed later.

2

SATAN, THE SON, THE WOMAN

The reader asks how an idea is born. He would like to know what to do to get there too. But he who has important things to say is in a hurry to express himself and cares little whether one knows the road he has traveled. Besides, the paths of knowledge are multiple, and only the goal is one. The divergences come from the fact that one often stops mid-way, or at some other point, and announces that he has arrived.

Now, no one has arrived if he has not stopped worrying about material life. None of those who believe that the supreme knowledge is given to improve life down here has arrived. That is the irrefutable sign, and don't ask us how we have operated if hunger still scares you, and sickness terrifies you.

No book read in a comfortable armchair can instruct, and no knowledge learned in order to shine can open the eyes.

If we speak, it is only because the hour has come, and the Divinity, which is triple and also one, requires that Its truth be proclaimed. It is a necessity for God, not for mankind.

The hour has sounded of which it is said: *Many are called, few are chosen.* But where are the chosen? We do not see them. . . . Who knows, perhaps just one is enough . . .

That is also a sign of imperfection: the fear of finding oneself alone.

But now we take up our subject, the leaves fall to the November wind, winter approaches, the seed has been sown in the vast plains of the North.

Satan and the Son, the second term of the Trinity, are one: two opposites in one, two poles of the same axis. He who bows before the Son bows before his enemy Satan, and he who goes to the black mass believes he is praying to Satan but he is praying to Christ, and in the shadow of souls the Black and the White find each other again in a single entwining.

Men have separated the Gentle Lamb from the tragic Abettor of Evil, because in their primary essence these two were separate. The law of the divine Breath willed it, and Jesus had the terrifying illumination of it when he cried out on the cross: *Oh! My Father, why have you abandoned me?*

The Father did not abandon the Son, it was the Son who detached himself, as is logical. But he who flees feels himself pushed on by an inescapable law, and that gives him the impression that he is being pushed away. He curses the law of flight, he becomes his own enemy.

Satan is on the horizontal line (see chapter 1), the will to stop. He says: "I myself am of divine essence. I will be God wherever I find myself. If my power is limited, it is because the Law pushes me beyond myself. So I will resist the Law, I will pluck the apple from its tree and, evolving in a spiral around myself from the depths of my center, I will vanquish God, I will be God."

It is on the horizontal line that this Thought is born. It maintains itself eternally, for everything is eternal in Divinity. Raise yourselves above yourselves to understand that.

But upon the horizontal line there *always* lives this other Thought as well: "I will go ahead, for I am imperfect. I will go farther, farther still, to the place where the Light is again found. There the Celestial Star shines, my haven is there, I will lead mankind there."

Obviously, he who, because of the law of the fall, is precipitated into the creation cannot conceive of his salvation outside of the salvation of the others. For the others are him, and he is the others. *The Father has not created anything without the Son, and all things exist through the Son;* this dogma is true.* But the Father does not need the others, who, anyway, are nothing, and that is why the Son endlessly begs the Father to accept them: *make them one in us, as we are One, You and I.*†

The Father has his law, as the Son has his. For the human brain this law is called Justice, and an iron rod symbolizes it. If one [person] suffices for the shining forth of the Light, one will be there. If several are needed, there will be several. A certain prophet foresaw that there would be one hundred forty-four thousand; what does it matter, because everything happens as it must. We, *La Flèche,* have received the order to say that a single woman suffices. We do not take pride in it, we write it to obey.

What then is needed? A very simple thing: for Satan to recognize himself in the Christ and that Christ in his turn should say: I was Satan . . . two brothers, a single essence.

Why a woman for this reconciliation? Why a woman to persuade the will-to-stop to accept the law of flight and also to convince him who has left the Father to return to the Father because the true path is the line that is oblique to the nature of Satan?

Why? Because, as we said in the first number of *La Flèche,* the divine Breath† traces by its movement the three sides of the triangle: from the culminating point the fall, from right to left, to the horizontal base and after running along this baseline, still from right to

---

*[Though not an exact quotation, this is reminiscent of Ephesians 3:9. —*Trans.*]
†[Apparently not a canonical quotation —*Trans.*]
‡[The Holy Spirit —*Trans.*]

left, the ascension back to the point of departure. This triple movement is eternal and included always at every point, but the profane
will never understand it. It suffices then for one to follow this statement according to the notion of time and of space.

The ascension on the line of return implies the harmonious
combination of the will-to-stop with the energy of the flight. This
fusion of the two opposing wills in a single new movement cannot
be achieved without the influence of a third force, and notably of
that, which, emanating directly from the Father, constitutes for the
double Son the irresistible attraction of the Woman. We said in our
first number why this force is of necessity feminine. It is the negative
of the Father, travel in the opposite direction: no longer from above
to below, but from below to above. It is essential to understand that.

In the projection of the divine into the human, that is to say in
human life, where everything is nothing more than repetition and
resemblance to the divine plan, the moment of the beginning of the
return [ascensional] movement must be symbolized, or consecrated,
by an analogous magical operation: a woman must become the
instrument of redemption for a man.

This is delicate to explain, and we need to open a parenthesis to
make clear what the shadows of the Christian era have obscured. We
must tell what purpose should be served, *so that all things may be
fulfilled,* by the union of the man and the woman on the bed of love.

All flesh is the condensation, or better, the immobilization
of spirit. All flesh is Satan; all life is the Son in flight. To accept
the flight and push back against the immobilization; that is what
the predestined woman must do: she who will mark the beginning of the new era in human history. This rite is formidable, for
it demands on the part of the woman a love of superhuman power
combined with capacity for renunciation that is no less unusual.

The woman who will place herself at the head of humanity for
the new march will adore the man who will be offered to her, will recognize in him the White and the Black, will absorb the White, will

keep it in the depths of her flesh a certain number of days (3,385), then, slowly and painfully, will detach herself from it. Then the Son, nourished by the flesh of the woman, will shine again through her discarnate, and the man who shall have served for this magic and in whom from then on there will remain only Black will suffer atrocious moral torments. The woman will see that and will rejoice, for thus the wound will be washed, and the Good separated from the Bad: the flight from the stopping.

In the womb of the woman, the spirit will have received the beneficial satanic (carnal) energy, and one will see at the end of the operation, after the 3,385 days, the male essence in the feminine substance.

The woman in whom this will be accomplished will dictate to the new generations the rites of the Religion of the Third Term.

We have used the future tense to describe all of that, but take note: these things are accomplished, and Satan is redeemed.

The divine magical operation of which we have just spoken has been carried out in the course of the last nine years. Exactly from the fourteenth of July 1921 to the twentieth of October 1930. This is what authorizes us to unveil the mystery, so that all those who are worthy of it should have their share of joy. There are beings who have suffered much during these nine years because, without knowing it, they were participating in the act of magical transubstantiation. Their vital energy was taken as a contribution. At present, peace is again upon them, and joy returns to their homes. And in the heavens the intermediary forces sing *Ave Maria*.

Humanity as a whole will feel the effect of the magical redemption little by little, with the establishment and diffusion of the new rites. On this subject one can profitably read the article of our friend and colleague Auguste Apôtre* on the black, white, and golden masses.

---

*[This is another of Naglowska's pseudonyms. The article referred to appears separately in this anthology. —*Trans.*]

3

LA FLÈCHE

THE MOTHER, THE VIRGIN, THE LOVER

To the three periods of the Breath of Life (see our lead article in *La Flèche* No. 1), which form on the plane of absolute reality the three aspects or the three simultaneous terms of the Trinity, correspond in the cycle—or as we prefer to say: in the triangle—to which we belong, three religions, or three successive *moral organizations* of humanity: the religion of Moses, the Christian religion, and the religion that is announced today under the sign of the arrow.

Considering these three religions from the point of view at which we have placed ourselves from the first number of our publication, they could be called: the religion of the Father, the religion of the Son, and the religion of the Woman, or that of the Holy Spirit or the Spirit of the flesh purified (liberated from satanic immobilization).

The religion of Moses, established on the ruins of the Egyptian pyramid, had organized the chosen people with a view to the veneration and the *translation upon earth* of the first term of the divine breath, the Father. We have said that this term is symbolized by the rod whose movement is descending, that is to say oriented from above to below. This was—it no longer is, for this religion today is nothing more than a pale memory—the organization that tended to sanctify the male and in the male the essential dynamism containing the origin of the generation of the Son. This religion, logically, saw in woman only the necessary complement to the father for the begetting of children, that is to say, the mother. That is why women were not accepted in the heart of the Israelite community until their first-born was circumcised, and the woman who had no sons was rejected because of that as being repudiated by God. For the same reason—the woman being admitted only as the mother of the son—the Israelite organization condemned adultery and left to the woman no possibility of life or personal development. Alongside of that and performing a meticulous triage among its men, the family of Israel prepared the male capable of pouring out into the woman the synthesis of his creative force in order to fecundate her miraculously (that is to say *magically,* for there is no longer any incomprehensible miracle for him who has attained the higher powers), and it is precisely this that happened for the holy virgin Mary: in the temple, while she humbly prayed, fully realizing her condition as obedient slave, the priest-mage touched the receptive point at the summit of her head and caused to penetrate into her the fluid of dynamic waves that, fertilizing her insides, gave her the perfect son, that is to say one definitively detached from the satanic will to cease about which we have spoken in numbers 1 and 2 of *La Flèche.* It was at this instant that there was born in the universe or upon the horizontal line of the divine Triangle, the Christic will, which is that of the liberation of pride from the detached fruit that wished to be God wherever it finds itself. At the same time, the Mosaic religion that prepared this event ceased to be useful to the Divinity, and the Jewish people quickly underwent the consequences: dispersion and degeneracy.

The Christian religion, organizing humanity with a view to the act of Redemption that consists, as we have said, in the harmonization or the reconciliation of the satanic immobilization with the christic fluidity, both duly polarized, has set up virginity as its supreme virtue because, while preparing the new human body by means of communion and the sacrament of marriage, it had to introduce into the world the mystical idea of extra-corporeal union accepted and consciously realized by the two sexes. As a transitional phase leading to this realization, the ideal of the virgin was imposed.

But at the present time this "purity," which is no such thing, has become useless, for we have entered into the third act of the Divine Comedy that requires of the human elite the realization of gnostic union, that is to say of this sublime marriage where the couple is formed for the purpose of making the celestial spark of divine knowledge shine forth from the contact of the two sexes. Today, the ideal is the lover who knows how to love her Beloved for the glory of the Christ-Satan reestablished in a single ascending unity reoriented toward the Father.

This marriage, this union, is not simply spiritual as some believe. It is a rite that also demands the cooperation of the body, for the deep flesh is the root of the spirit, and the divine energy touches the man and the woman in the organs concerning which they feel shame. Justifiably shame, because for centuries they have been making a scandalous use of them. Note this well: it is not the organ that is shameful, but the ill will of the humans who make use of it for themselves and not for God.

It is at this point that one will recognize the chosen: they will quiver with joy on reading this passage, while the others, the bad ones, will clench their teeth in rage and impotence, and drool will run from their mouth. For they will recognize the truth of what we are advancing, but they will also recognize that this virtue is forever refused to them. They will sink into their vices, and from time to time they will throw themselves into the abyss of the nether realms. One will see then, one sees it already, an atrocious cretinization of humankind; idiocy and weakness of spirit will be the share of many, and before long there will be a new species of which it will be difficult to say whether it is simian or human.

And nothing can prevent this frightening tumble, for we are at the day of the final divine judgment, and the Savior has marked on the forehead, between the two eyes, those who will go with him.

Miraculously (magically), some can still be saved, but on the superhuman condition of a sincere renunciation of pride.

Examine your conscience, my brothers, ask yourselves this question: "Are you capable of making yourself neutral in the face of an offense to the point of letting it slide through you like a stone through the water? Are you capable of letting yourselves be sullied without sullying yourselves? Can you live as if the opinion of the people around you did not exist?"

If you can answer "yes" in all honesty, continue on to this other, definitive question: "Would you be able to renounce the pleasure of sex at the exact moment of enjoyment? Would you be able to transform this *enjoyment* into the *joy* of supreme knowledge?"

To forget oneself without forgetting oneself, to offer oneself without offering oneself, to love without loving, to suffer without suffering, to let the triple breath of divine life live in one, that is what is necessary, for all the rest is nothing but hindrance and silly vanity.

4

LA FLÈCHE

HELL AND THOSE
PUNISHED

Today we take up the most delicate point of our doctrine: the application, or more exactly the *translation* of the charter of the Third Term of the Trinity into human life.

This point is difficult to treat because, throughout the decadent era of materialism, brains have become too habituated to considering every problem, divine or human, in light of the elementary needs of the body, to such an extent that many people do not feel that they have understood something in the philosophical or metaphysical realm unless the proposed solution gives the impression of immediately opening up a new horizon in one of these three areas: eating, earning, or playing at love. Every argument that demands that one forget the sphere of one's habitual activity in order to understand that which is being presented seems, to those (alas, too numerous) brains, to be a march into indecipherable shadows.

This sad state of affairs has been unfortunate for many of the *Words* launched into the world in recent years. To *facilitate* understanding of the divine region, to widen the circle of the fervent around the great ideas, many groups, and first among them the Theosophical Society founded by Madame Blavatsky and directed after her death by Annie Besant, have prostituted the divine by cutting it into small pieces of cake that are easy to digest, and have surrounded the great Central Enigma that they proposed to unveil (for such was the order that had been given them) with a veil thicker than the one before . . . in order not to offend the weak and fearful!

The service that they have thus rendered to the Cause may be easily guessed: Isis of the fecund womb is presented to the world in a more degraded state than ever, and her priests and priestesses, to take in money today to do good tomorrow, as they claim, talk nonsense and preach foolishness, putting the adepts to sleep in a blessed inertia whose chief element is self-satisfaction. One does not ask any real effort of the people who approach the altars, any recognition of their inferiority, any realization of their fall. The great consolation of *Karma* takes care of everything: you are weak today, you will be strong in a future life; you are all poor now, you will be rich at another time, in another body, beneath other skies; you can be neither priest nor prince, because you lack the qualities, you will have what it takes for these dignities in another existence when your *Karma* has run out. Because of this, and each one aiming only for the final goal of a king's throne, each theosopher feels himself the equal of all, and by anticipation already the future King of Kings. That behind all this there should be something to *realize* in the matter of the definitive reintegration of all in the All, and a whole long gravitation around the Invisible, that is easily cut down in brains now calmed concerning the main thing, which is their self-love. The bottom line is that justice has been rendered to all and each is "great," since all will be, someday. It's only a question of time, and long live Theosophy!

But the great Blavatsky, if she came back today to her disciples, would have reason to be frightened. She had taken enormous pains to announce everywhere the end of one era and the upcoming beginning of a new slice of history. She had sown to harvest today fruits that, in the meantime, should have ripened, but to be sure, it is not among the theosophers that she would have to look to find them. As always, the roses have bloomed outside of the chapel, and he who would now like to form the sheaf of the chosen must begin again the wearisome voyages to reunite what time has scattered.

Still, the chosen are there and the sheaf will be formed, we do not hesitate to proclaim it loudly. We know that they are there, and we know that they will group themselves, attracted to each other by an unknown force that will not ask them for their consent, because the good must finally be separated from the bad.

Those, the good, will understand what we are writing, and perhaps even beyond what the letters can express. It is for them that we say what follows:

The translation of the charter of the Third Term of the Trinity into human life is a new realization of sexual love. It is no longer two bodies that take each other to make merry, but two beings of different sexes who approach each other with a special religiosity and according to a particular rite to cause the divine spark of knowledge to shine forth from their contact.

This operation, this rite is of such nature that it leaves no place for the regard of self-love. He who fails, fails cleanly, visibly, indisputably, and he who succeeds, succeeds similarly precisely, without any possible shadow of misunderstanding.

The one who is victorious in the test, comes out of it spiritually fortified and as if illuminated, and the new faculties added from then on to his intelligence and his will cannot be denied by any observer. The hierarchy of worth is thus established in a peremptory way, and the obedience of the inferior to the superior becomes natural.

This is the basis of the new pyramid that we are preaching, and whose inevitable construction we foresee. The society that will be organized on the ruins of that which is decomposing today will be formed by its new people, regenerated by the new fire of love, and the work that they accomplish will necessarily be good and efficacious.

What disturbs certain sorrowful spirits today, when one talks to them about these things, is the idea that at the wide lower levels of the new Pyramid, one will have to expect a whole army of shadowy beings, lacking in intelligence, whose incapacity itself will reduce to the role of simple slaves. But don't we know that the materially unhappy fate of human societies comes precisely from the policy exercised with regard to the incapable? Don't we know that everything gets muddled and obscured when, in order not to offend a person of little capability we entrust to him anyway the role of governor? It is because the last century exercised this policy to excess that we are now in a general chaos from which all suffer.

The new era will not know the demoralizing catering to everything that is unworthy.

The new era will not be based on the false idea that each one must be flattered and adulated apart from his merit.

Besides, with the divine light shining into the world, every man will concern himself much less with himself than with the Eternal Truth, which will again become a living factor in life, and every woman will know that her role is not to be a little queen next to a meager brook, but a priestess illuminated by vivifying love.

When women know that, when their sacred mission is taught to them from a young age, the current plague of immorality will disappear naturally. No woman, unless she is a monster, will be able to give herself to prostitution, and one will no longer do in secret the abominable things that one does now, for one will know, as one knows that one is upon the earth, that the comedy of love without love and magic is a crime that nature cannot forgive, even if people are indulgent.

For as we have said in our preceding numbers, the era of the translation of the charter of the Third Term of the Trinity is the era of redemption, the epoch of the definitive utilization of the good energies and the parallel condemnation of the refractory forces.

Everything that does not serve the rectification according to the divine will for the reorientation toward God of the energy entrusted to humans, will be cast into the lower realms and that is the hell predicted by the prophets: a hell on earth and with the punished in flesh and blood in the full light of the sun.

It is unfortunate that one cannot persuade each one of this while there is still time, and death can still be avoided and replaced by life.

It is still more unfortunate to know the way and not be able to lead all humanity on this path to save it. But how does one cure those who do not recognize that they are ill? How does one call to God those who do not believe in his reality and how does one keep from drowning those who do not see the floodwaters leaving their overflowed banks in menacing tides?

The sufferings of humanity will be fearsome because its ill will is without limit.

[The chapter continues now, in *La Flèche* No. 5.]

Our friend and collaborator Auguste Apôtre finished his last article, in *La Flèche* No. 4, by saying:

It is the West that knows the Truth, it is from the West that our salvation will come to us.

We are in perfect agreement with him, and today we will lay out the reasons that cause us to affirm that the path that has led humanity toward the translation of the charter of the Third Term of the Trinity on earth, whose principal characteristic is the realization of gnostic love, of the love that causes divine knowledge to shine forth from the contact of two bodies, has been Christianity such as we know it through its history.

We emphasize these last words in order to separate ourselves cleanly from those who make a distinction between the word of Christ and the theological teaching given by the Roman Catholic Church and the Orthodox Catholic Church (called Greek), in pretending that the truth was in the mouth of the Christ but that it has been unrecognized by the Church.

No, we argue that the two Churches that we have just mentioned have given to the world what they were supposed to give and that Saint Peter as well as Saint Andrew built the house of God on earth exactly as they should have, for Jesus said to John: "You, follow me," and then immediately to Peter: "Don't concern yourself with what this one will do."*

Peter and Andrew, the protectors of the Roman Church and the Byzantine Church (Russian in particular) did not occupy themselves with what John was doing, in the course of the past nineteen centuries, and they did well not to. For their duty was to lead all of humanity to the threshold of the third temple, the temple that we will build now, and whose secret has been entrusted by the Man-God precisely to John.

It is in the just accomplishment of this task of universal character, catholic, that the merit of Christianity resides, such as we know it through its history, and we repeat again that no religion—we do well to say *no*—has spread through the world a doctrine and (magical) practices better suited to the goal of the universal elevation of humanity toward those spiritual regions that confer upon humans the capacity to make sublime the vital force hidden in the organ of which they are ashamed because they abuse it scandalously, and to make divine that which is carnal.

The Church has never unveiled its true magical action for the profane, because it was not yet time and because it was necessary—as we have already said—to first introduce to humanity the ideal of virginity to accustom humans, down through the centuries, to conceive of something other than procreation, ideal of the First Term symbolized by the Rod (concerning this, reread our articles in numbers 1 and 2 of *La Flèche*), whose religion, or translation on the earth, was Judaism.

But at present, and without an official proclamation of the Church even being necessary, one clearly sees leaving the bosom of

---

*[This seems to be intended as a paraphrase of John 21:19–22. —*Trans.*]

the latter certain elite spirits (not those who are known, but those that one meets by chance on the roads) who, in the face of the ideas coming from the Indies, have the right to say: "Stop right there! Don't come to confound our work, putting old things back on the table that cannot serve the present reconstruction."

For today it is no longer a matter of offering the means of individual perfection to humans—work of the Orient—but of building a new religion or moral organization as the basis of a new civilization, capable of leading the human collectivity toward the celestial regions: work and goal of the West.

And it is precisely in that that the triangle, to which we belong like masons to the work, is distinguished from the "wisdom" of the Orient.

Our triangle—the Jewish and Christian religions and the one that we shall establish shortly—has put forth since its first period the principle of the purification of the collectivity by the common and hierarchically coordinated effort of all. Since Moses, and only from the time of Moses, the world has known the meaning of the sanctity of a nation that collectively makes a continuing effort for perfection with the goal of the realization of the Ideal Man, of the Messiah *who will change all things, because all things shall become new through Him.**

Christianity has rendered this principle universal, it has catholicized it, while going beyond the limits of nationalism, which it has replaced by the idea of the brotherhood of all men, and it has invited all humanity to the future realization of the Kingdom of Heaven on earth. But the fundamental idea stayed the same: the salvation, the regeneration, will come into the world through the First, and this First will be forged by all. It is by the effort of Humanity, understood as an entity, by the *Church,* that all the preparatory things will be accomplished.

And today those things are accomplished. The churches have

---

*[This is an echo of Revelation 21:4–5. —*Trans.*]

done what they had to do. The hour has sounded. The King of kings arrives.

Useless is the effort of those who, getting drunk on oriental extravagances, wish to point people to individual paths. Those small roads, narrow and tortuous, do not lead to the main road, and those who are not there will not reach it in time. As we have already said, repeating what is written, there will be a destruction *en masse* of all the *unjust,* of all those who have not accepted in their heart and realized in their body the two preceding stages: the strengthening by the Rod and the purification by the Cross.

They will not return to the earth to take up again the path of evolution but will be cast into involution, and they will descend by stages into the lower kingdoms: animal, vegetable, mineral, from which a return is definitely problematic.

Today it is a matter of everyone standing up and raising their eyes toward the same Star. Those who don't will perish.

It is written in the Holy Scriptures that at the end of times an order will be given to the protector of the Temple: "Check the building and do not allow anything to subsist except that which is holy; the rest must be cast down immediately."

We are at the end of times, and the guardians of the Temple are checking its walls.

When the triage is finished, when the good are separated from the unworthy, the Third Temple, the one where the symbol will be replaced by life, will be founded in the very heart of the present Temple. It is thus that the Religion of Suffering will become the Religion of Glory.

5

LA FLÈCHE

THE THIRD TEMPLE

When the Temple of the Third Term of the Trinity is erected the men will arrange themselves there in three distinct groups. For there will be the witnesses of the first era, the Jews; the witnesses of the second era, the Christians and the Satanists; and the witnesses of the New Charter, the Ternaries.

The lukewarm and the colorless will place themselves in the courtyard.

The men of the first two groups will constitute what we shall call the *presence of the Past around the Future,* and their role will be to call to mind for the priests of the Ascension the wisdom of the Descent (*First Term*) and the merit of the Suffering (*Second Term*).

Homage and honor will be rendered to both.

The witnesses of the first and the second hours will not participate actively in the rites of the Third Term, but they will hold in their right hand the lighted torch of *their* truth.

Their thought will be: "We persist, so that all things may be present at the hour of the closing of the Triangle, at the hour when the Angel of Death will cut down with its scythe all the bad vegetation. For the Sun still shines for the good and the bad, and many souls can still be saved. We are the guardians of the past, we are those who slow the haste of the future."

And, indeed, the catastrophe foreseen for 1933 will not be definitive.

There will be another one, still more terrible, when the line of the Ascension, begun today, shall have been traced in the divine Cosmos up to its junction with the point of departure of the Fall.

Then, as it is written in the Holy Scriptures, the spirit of destruction will be unchained and sent among humans to destroy by new carnage, still worse than the preceding, all of the remaining rot.

Then the weeping and gnashing of teeth will not mollify anyone, for no regenerated soul will keep the illusions of the fruits fallen to earth, nor will believe in the usefulness of those who have not entered into the Cone of the new life.

And having no more saints to pray for them, the evil ones will die without hope of rebirth.

In the Temple of the Third Term the priests and priestesses of the Ascension will accomplish the act of deliverance.

One will choose seven men and three women, healthy in spirit, heart, and body, and one will have them accomplish the act of love for the regeneration of humankind.

This will be a solemn rite, preceded by chants and music and discourses in conformity with the new truth, and one will drink the wine of celebration to indicate to all that this rite is a joy that crowns long sorrows.

The high priestess, announcer of the new Term, will signal the beginning and the end of the rite to those assembled, and through her the divine energy, liberated due to the contact of the bodies in the sanctuary, will be spread over the congregation.

The men and women who participate in the rite will experience a great moral and spiritual benefit from it, and their own vital energy will be fortified and sanctified by it.

But, obviously, one will not accomplish this great magical rite in ordinary nuptial chambers, nor in any place where individual egotism reigns.

The ritual love of the priests and priestesses of the Ascension has nothing in common with the habitual practices of mortals, and it is necessary to belong to the spiritual head of humanity to conceive of it.

In the meantime it is necessary that, beginning from today, the world should be instructed in these things, so that the head may grow and the body profit thereby. The head and the body of Humanity:

"LA FLÈCHE"

The lines that one has just read constitute a fragment of the text that we shall publish with the title "The New Ternary Rites,"* once the material conditions—which always depend upon the spiritual and occult conditions—lend themselves to it.

We give them here, as also the page that follows, to launch into the world in this month of March the first sounds of the new music.

We hope that our readers will understand and appreciate our intention.

We hope that this first seed will fall on fertile ground and that the souls that receive it will allow the beautiful plant of the future to grow within them.

In human terms—oh! How reluctantly we return to those terms!— the plant of the future is that of frankness, justice, and rectitude. It brings Peace, for it reduces constraint, the source of hatred and strife.

In divine terms—and at this moment we would like to shake the hands of those who understand us—the new plant signifies the new love. On this plane it brings Deliverance.

M. de N.

---

*[So far as is known, the work was never published. —*Trans.*]

PART II

other religious and philosophical writings

❧

White masses, black masses, golden masses . . . how to become a magus . . . the Kabbalah . . . the golden mass of the sabbath . . . the polarization of the sexes . . . pharaonic and phallic truths in Randolph . . . the individual soul . . . the priestesses of the future . . . a magical séance . . . the key of Saint Peter . . . satanism . . . an open letter to Pope Pius XI . . . initiatic eroticism . . . these are just some of the fascinating articles in this second part of our anthology.

6

WHITE MASSES, BLACK MASSES, GOLDEN MASSES

This is a very little-known article in any language, because it appeared in La Flèche *No. 2, the rarest of all the issues, which was completely sold-out in the 1930s, while Naglowska was still publishing the newspaper. Naglowska signed this article with one of her favorite noms-de-plume, Auguste Apôtre.*

❧⊰◈⊱❧

The Catholic Mass, as one should know, is a magical operation that binds to Christ (to the Desire to Return to the Father) every communicant, independently of the latter's wish.

In taking in the transubstantiated bread, every living being receives, in effect, the christic dynamism introduced into the communion bread by the *mystery* of the eucharist, and this dynamism immediately works in the body in an efficacious fashion for the task imposed by the official Church: the preparation of the material possibility of the coming to earth of the glorious Christ, that is to say for the resumption of direct contact between humanity and divinity. In this sense, the Church effectively redeems the people, that is to say the body of Christ, and she is right to tend toward universality, for as said in *La Flèche,* the escaping Son wishes the liberation of all.

At the same time, this work of the Church prepares the possibility of the magical operation of redemption (see above), for the slow penetration of the christic dynamism into humanity is necessary, through the ages and the generations, for the accomplishment in their fullness of the rites of the Golden Mass, of which we shall speak below.

This truth is only rarely taught in the bosom of the Orthodox Catholic Church, and the Roman Church has been carefully hiding it for centuries, because the psychic element brought by the faithful gathered together at the religious ceremony is a powerful factor for the preparation of the transubstantiation and, obviously, the fervor of the public would be much less if each one knew that he had been invited to the mass for something from which he will derive no individual benefit, either spiritual or material, given that it concerns an event that will be produced when he has long been in the grave.

It is even to radically impede any knowledge relative to the future reappearance of the flesh of the woman of the sublime discarnate Spirit, and to thus keep intact the faith of the peoples, that the Roman clergy decided, at the beginning of the dark era, to cruelly exterminate, by sword and by fire, the initiates of the secret societies. Every person of any culture knows the story of these cruelties; it is therefore useless for us to speak about them at greater length.

Still, if cruelty there has been, the Roman Church does not stand any the less in *its truth,* for men do only what they must do, and the role of the Roman Church, the Church of Peter, was precisely that of preparing the flesh without worrying about the spirit. *You will build my church, and it will last until my return,* Jesus said to the apostle Peter, *what John shall do does not concern you.*

The spirit, since the death of the Master, has received the order to carefully hide, and the men to whom the *tradition* was entrusted swore to guard its secret until the day when the predestined woman should be born. They transmitted the hidden teaching from mouth to ear conscientiously up to our epoch. At present the secret must be unveiled, because the Woman is there, and because things have been accomplished as they had to be. Today, it is necessary to render homage to all those who have worked in the shadows to prevent the extinction of the divine flame in the course of the dark age of the preparation of the body. Their task has been hard, and their devotion admirable, for they knew that they themselves were destined for death. They kept its symbol in their chapels, and said upon entering "I am dying . . . I die so that the Other may live again."

In sum, what did those men do? Many accessory things with a goal of discipline and self-preparation, and one essential thing: the operation that is called the Black Mass and which, by the passage of the satanic dynamism (the spirit of immobilization) of the sperm of the man into the soul of the woman, prepares, equally through the ages and generations, the magical will of the woman with a view to the liberating Conception explained by *La Flèche* in the article that you have just read [the last section of the Book of Life].

Thus, therefore, the official Church and the invisible Church have both worked for the preparation of the new era. The usefulness of the two of them ceases today, that is why we note an obvious decadence among Catholics as well as among occultists. That which no longer serves falls to pieces and rots.

Today, the hour of the Redemption has sounded, and the new generations are called to new things. A new organization begins, new rites will be instituted.

What must be done is to attract the greatest possible number of humans around the table of the Spouse, who invites everyone to benefit from His joy. We are living in an epoch of transition; it is the period in which the Son sends his emissaries to gather the mature fruit. Woe to those who are not ready! They will perish, they are perishing already. That is the reason for the wars and the crimes from which we suffer. Let us hasten to give the remedy to Humanity, sick from giving birth, let us hasten to tell it what the Golden Mass is.

It is certainly a part of magic, just as the White (Catholic) Mass is, and the (occultist) Black Mass, but totally without being either one or the other it has parts of the two at one time: the Golden Mass offers to communicants the dynamism of the ascension. The tradition, that is to say the transmission, has not yet begun, since only yesterday the march took shape and only one is there who can offer the new apple. But the formula is dictated and the new rite is ordained.

It is necessary that twelve pure ones should meet in a room around the woman who henceforth alone has the power to reverse in them the direction of desire. These twelve shall then be consecrated, and they will become the first twelve priests of the new Church.

Their *blood* shall be from that time the sacred element that the adepts will mix with theirs to acquire the rhythm of taking flight: the red blood taken from their right and introduced into the left arm of the adepts.

But a special training and *culture* will precede the operation, for impurity is great among men. For the rest, three years are granted to us before the definitive triage. Three years are nothing in the face of eternity.

7

LA FLÈCHE

THE TWO RIVERBANKS

"The Two Riverbanks" appeared in La Flèche *No. 3, 15 Dec. 1930. This short piece, full of symbolic language, seems to be about an initiatic experience that Naglowska has had. The ideas presented in it are close to those in* The Sacred Rite of Magical Love. *It was signed "Us," but I have no doubt that Naglowska wrote it herself.*

❈

There are two banks and a river between the two.

He who is here is not there and, therefore, does not know anything about what happens over there. He talks about it anyway, according to what he believes, and he prophesies and he counsels. But you, listen to your own reason, for that is all that can convince you.

In the meantime, lend a curious ear to the reports of the others, but know that they are only reports, and that, for you, their value cannot be absolute.

It is useful to know what others are saying, certainly, but reject what you cannot accept, and do not be a hypocrite.

Here is the report of one of those who has been there.

There is the marriage of the first bank, and there is the marriage of the second bank, and these two are not the same. If you are on the first bank, accomplish the marriage of the first bank, and say that the second bank and its different marriage do not exist. Obey the Law and do nothing more.

But I, who have gone there, am telling you: the marriage of the second bank exists and that one is truly indissoluble, because there the man and the woman create a god who is their son but who is them at the same time. You know well that water is made from acid and its generating principle. May this fact guide you for the understanding of this mystery.

But if you haven't seen that, say that it never was and say also that it will never be, because above all, guard yourself from being a hypocrite.

On the second bank, that is to say after the long and terrible crossing of the river, the man is different and the woman is different and what they can do then is something else . . .

But say that it doesn't exist, if you are not able to conceive of it.

On the second bank, the *fire* does not burn but it vivifies, being a source of continuous creation, and the son does not become crystallized, for he does not die.

And not becoming dead flesh, he does not keep the father and the mother in separation, but he unites them continually in a single unity that is triple and immortal.

Say that none of that exists, if you do not conceive of it . . .

The immortal unity, created in this manner by the man and the woman of the second bank, is *visible* to all those who have new eyes, and the word of the god re-created is perceptible to their ears . . .

But do not believe those who tell lies. There are many, and they are still multiplying . . .

There are two banks and a river between the two.

There are those who believe that the river is death and that the second bank is a life in another body. Others believe many other things, but I who have gone there, I tell you: the river is in life and not in death, and he who crosses it is living flesh and not a shadow. That is why I repeat: one crosses the river while living or one does not cross it at all . . .

Still, there is no obligation for anyone to attempt that dangerous passage, and it is better to be honest and to die honest than to be a hypocrite and die in hypocrisy and pretense . . .

There is a second bank, I tell you, and another power in this other *land*.

Do not go there if you do not have the strength.

8

TO BECOME A MAGUS

This short piece is from La Flèche *No. 4, January 15, 1931. It carries no signature line, but it is stated in the listing of contents on the front page of this issue that it was written by "Auguste Apôtre" (one of Naglowska's pseudonyms).*

We are well aware that the ambition to become a Magus is noble and praiseworthy if its goal is real and positive knowledge of the great truths of the beyond.

But it seems to us that any magical practice that tends to the acquisition of special powers just to place the practitioner above others and so to attract to himself material advantages, is nothing but low sorcery. And this is not because the appetite would be worthy of condemnation in itself, but because the egotistic care that it presupposes is by definition a hindrance to knowledge.

Indeed, he who tries to penetrate the divine secrets to make use of them himself limits his horizon and, placed before the vast perspectives of the celestial plains, instead of merging into them, he shrinks them together in himself instead and reduces the Infinite to a single imperceptible point: the personal "me."

Such a Magus, even if he accomplishes miracles, remains a limited man, and his knowledge will never have any other effectiveness than that of some occupation or other more or less well exercised. Perhaps it will be a practical means of human combat, but it will never have the value of true creation.

For divine Magic, that which opens the gates of the eternal Temple where the fire of fecund Love burns without ever being extinguished, is not an accessory faculty acquired by the practitioner, but the result of an organic development that transforms the student from that which he is into that which he becomes: from a man with limited sight to one with unlimited sight, and from a man with partial comprehension to a man with total comprehension, from a man of impotent love to a man with love that creates.

Certainly, the roads traveled by one magician and another will not be the same, and the preparatory practices to which they dedicate themselves differ considerably.

While the future sorcerer practices with indifference, like a placid surgeon, gymnastics and respiratory methods that are more or less complicated, carefully choosing the foods that he absorbs, the student of divine magic begins his apprenticeship with a long education of his heart and his intelligence. First he acquires the moral virtues, above all those that accustom him to forgetting himself as easily as possible. Not because forgetting himself would be a special merit that would attract to itself a special recompense, but because this forgetting is one of the necessary and sufficient conditions for a real embrace of what is beyond the habitual possibilities of people. It is not a condition of moral attractiveness, but a necessity inherent to flight into the sublime regions itself.

The student of divine magic will exercise his intelligence with disinterested penetration of theological and metaphysical problems, strengthening as much as possible his logic and his capacity to understand theses that are located outside of his habitual life, first of all because abstract intelligence is necessary for penetration into Magic, and also because caring about problems concerning invisible things purifies a person of his egotism and, as a result, contributes to his liberation from heavy physical laws.

The student of divine magic will devote himself, finally, to prolonged and often-repeated meditations, to awaken within himself the vibrations of the celestial regions, in such a way that the life that surrounds us and extends beyond us should be at the base of his being like real music or scenery. Little by little he will thus acquire the poetic faculty that is first among the qualities of a Magus.

9

THE KABBALAH

This article is from La Flèche *No. 5, February 15, 1931. It was* signed *"M. de N."*

꘎

Under the auspices of the Friends of the magazine *Symbolism* and under the honorary direction of Master Oswald Wirth, there took place, the other day, in the hall of "La Raison," 46, rue Ramey, a very interesting conference on "The Theoretical and Practical Kabbalah," given by Mr. Grajewski, formerly a professor at the Rabbinical School.

The conference-presenter, whom we, however, reproach for having excessively exercised brains that fear fatigue, made it clear that, while Talmudists must be considered to be cold commentators on the Mosaic Law, Kabbalists deserve to be treated as artists.

Mr. Grajewski has even said very felicitously: "One becomes a Talmudist by patient studies, but to be a Kabbalist, one must be born so."

And, indeed, the Kabbalah, full of ingenious demonstrations based on the most unexpected joinings and separatings of the 22 Hebrew letters, which are combined with other signs to reach a total of 72, is like a series of algebraic poems that one can neither conceive of nor assimilate without great imaginative power.

But that is no doubt what gives it its charm, and it is certainly what proves the superiority of its creators: for imagination is the first virtue of man that allows him to cure his terrestrial myopia.

Pressed by the questions posed to him at the end of his speech, Mr. Grajewski allowed that at the period when the Kabbalists, moved by the persecutions inflicted on the Jewish people, conceived the reckless project of hastening the coming of the Messiah, Savior of Israel, to confound their enemies, they discovered, always by their method of composition and decomposition of sacred signs, the great secret of the transmutation of animal energy into spiritual energy, which transmutation is none other than the act of magical love known by the magicians of Egypt and advocated today by *La Flèche.*

Naturally, the very proper lecturer affirmed all of this only in cryptic words so as not to disturb the many ladies who had come to this wonderful talk.

If he had been bolder—and his great erudition certainly permitted him this—Mr. Grajewski would perhaps have told us why the efforts both sincere and grandiose of the Kabbalists had not produced the desired result. Why had the Messiah not come in those Middle Ages that were so cruel to the Jews? Why had the acquired transmutation of energies—and it was, if not the Kabbalists would not have known it so well—not taken on the proportions of a definitive world and cosmic event?

We do not know the opinion of Mr. Grajewski on this subject, but we believe that what the Kabbalists were lacking in the Middle Ages was *God's consent.*

For a man can by his own effort accomplish his individual transmutation, but in order for this operation to have a world-saving value, it is necessary that *the time should have come for it,* that is to say it is necessary that the *divine comedy* that is played through all humanity should be in harmony with what humans do.

And here is our conclusion. Given that today we are at the Angle of the ternary, it is only today that a man can become Man-God by the magic of love, as Jesus did by the magic of spiritual birth. But for this to take place there is need for a collectivity desiring it.

La Flèche was born to provoke this desire.

10

THE COMMANDMENTS Of THE THIRD TERM Of THE TRINITY

This list of the commandments of Naglowska's new religion was published in La Flèche *No. 6, March 15, 1931. A different list was published in* The Light of Sex[1] *approximately a year and a half later. This earlier version has much to recommend it.*

⸙

The Commandments of the Third Term of the Trinity

1. You will recognize God in yourself and around you and in the whole Universe, for all that is visible and invisible is the result of the Life of God, the only being that can say, "I am."

    The flesh says, "I was and I will be." Life says, "I am."

2. You will recognize yourself as the servant of Life, your God, or of God, your Life, and you will not adore any visible or invisible

intermediate force, for whoever adores an intermediate force belongs to that intermediate force and perishes with it when its time has expired.

Belong to Him who is, and not to him of whom one will say, "he was."

3. Do not give any name to your God (= Life), because a name is a prison and God has no walls.

The name begins with the breath, and the breath passes and is repeated in another time, always the same, endlessly different.

No name is eternal, how can you give one to Him who continues on?

4. You will build a temple to adore your God (= your Life), for your cares are impure, and you need a place to enter into, washed of your cares.

11

THE GOLDEN MASS OF THE SABBATH

This is an extremely important article for Naglowska studies. It was published in La Flèche *No. 6, March 15, 1931, and it gives the fullest account that exists of Naglowska's Golden Mass. Naglowska signed it "by order of the Cone, M. de N." The inclusion of the mention of the "Cone," which in Naglowska's symbolic language indicated a higher power, gives it an extra sense of formality. She also wrote "à suivre" ("to be continued"), but such continuation unfortunately never happened. On the same page with the article, there is an advertisement for a "special publication" of* La Flèche, *which was to appear under the title* Les nouveaux Rites ternaires *(The New Ternary Rites). The ad stated that the promised work would "contain the details" of the rite spoken of in the article.*

~❧❧~

You will come into the Temple on the evening of the Sabbath, in the night that separates and unites the time of rest of the Jews, the

Witnesses, and the time of rest of the Christians, the Sacrificers.

You will stay there for three hours with your brothers and the chosen of your Mother, and you will give thanks: from eleven o'clock to midnight to Moses, the founder of the Witnessing, and from midnight to one o'clock to Jesus, the Establisher of the Sacrifice, and from one o'clock to two o'clock to the Life liberated from the prison of the flesh.

If you are profane, you will place yourself among the profane, your brothers, and you will listen and you will receive with them as long as you have not been initiated.

If you are initiated, you will place yourself among the initiates. From eleven o'clock to midnight on the right, if you are circumcised, and on the left if you are not. At midnight the circumcised will pass to the left, ceding their places to the uncircumcised.*

The initiated women will place themselves in the middle of the hall, between the circumcised and the uncircumcised. They shall line up one behind the other, and they shall enter into the Temple veiled with three veils; the first veil shall be white, the second black, the third red.

The women shall keep their three veils on from eleven o'clock to midnight, at which time they shall take off the red veil. The second veil shall be removed at the end of the second hour of their attendance, and the third during the ceremony of the last hour, between one and two o'clock in the morning.

For the red belongs to the flesh that is blessed, the black to the sorrow of the separation, and the white to the joy of the renewal.

During the first hour of attendance you will commemorate the formation of the people of Israel and the symbol of the pact concluded between God and his chosen people: the Rod hidden in the Ark.

---

*[In the original French text we find here the following additional stipulation, which I believe Naglowska would not have included today: "You will not introduce into your midst any man of black or red color, for these races are expired." —*Trans.*]

The women shall remain silent, with their gaze turned toward the ground. They shall not make any movement, and their attitude will call to mind the obedience of the women of the first era.

The men will sing canticles and listen to the discourse of the chief, and they will recite several times the following formula:

"When Moses traversed the Red Sea our triangle began, and the woman was submissive to the man, her husband, to procreate according to the Law. We give thanks to the phase of blessed childbirth, and we keep the respectful memory of it."

Each time that this formula shall be pronounced by the initiated men, the chief will say to the Christians:

"Salute the witnesses of the first era."

The Christians will turn toward the Jews and will make three solemn bows.

The Jews will answer the salute, saying: "We are your brothers."

The chief will then trace with his sword the triangle of life and will say:

"It was the Rod, that became the Sword, it is now the Arrow."

This formula shall be pronounced at the beginning, in the middle, and at the end of the first hour.

It will be pronounced the last time at midnight and the women shall then prostrate themselves on the ground. The men will pass over the women, the Jews ceding their place, on the right, to the Christians, to arrange themselves at the left of the hall.

At the stroke of midnight the chief shall order the women [who had prostrated themselves] to arise, saying:

"Women, arise! Remove the veil of blood and appear in our midst black from shame. For the hour of the benediction has passed and we are now entering the era of suffering. Behold the sword that is placed between you and the Man who rejects you for his purification by suffering."

At this moment, from the left and from the right, swords will be launched in the direction of the women. They will fall to the ground, forming a separation between the men and the women.

Then a group will detach itself from the circumcized and from the uncircumcised. These men will drape themselves in red, seize the swords lying on the ground, and will turn them against those who launched them.

A fight will ensue. This will be war.

The women shall retire to the back of the hall. They will tear away their red veils and will wrap the black veil tightly around themselves.

They will take up the following chant:

> *Behold before us the desolate sea and the pale horizon*
> *   that beckons to a voyage.*
> *Let us go up, one by one, into the trembling ships and*
> *   let us entrust our fate to these waves.*
> *The divine Groom has lost his Bride, their suffering*
> *   moans in us.*
> *Let us weep their far-off tears, perhaps we shall find*
> *   again their rose.*

And while the men inflict tortures upon themselves, the women, veiled in black, will skirt the walls of the hall in single file.

When they are close to the curtain separating the hall of the audience from the Sanctuary of the Act, the Mother, who is there to attend them, will give out to each of them a lighted torch.

She will ask questions and receive the following answers:

QUESTION 1. My sisters, what have you seen in the course of this voyage?

ANSWER: We have seen furious waves in the sea and on the shores men who are lost.

QUESTION 2. What did the waves tell you, and what did the men tell you?

ANSWER: The waves are mute, and the men are unconscious. Neither have told us anything worthwhile.

QUESTION 3. What do you wish to know, my sisters and my daughters?

ANSWER: The truth about the Birth, the truth about the Suffering, and the truth about the Vision of the Day. For the Birth is accomplished in us, the Suffering is prolonged through us, but the Vision of the Day is done outside of us.
The Birth of the Son, what is that for us?
There will then be a deep silence in the hall, the fighting will stop, and the men will sing in chorus:

> *While war was in us and around us, see, the women*
> *   accomplished a voyage.*
> *Let us bless the war, the struggle, and the tortures,*
> *   for here are our sisters at the threshold of the*
> *   Sanctuary.*
> *Dressed in black and in tears, they have felt the mystery.*
> *   They want to know the reason that causes us, that*
> *   unites us to them and separates us from them.*
> *Blessed be the night that saddens and inspires.*

After that the men shall arrange themselves without distinction between circumcised and uncircumcised, and the women shall place themselves in the first row, with the lighted torches in their hands.
The Mother will say this:
"The first hour was that of the Marriage, that of the descent of divinity into humanity for the spiritual fecundation of the latter.
The animal became Man.
The second hour was that of the war and the Separation, for the fertilized mother, Humanity, had to let mature in her the fruit of the Marriage.

At present the Son of Man is within us, and the third hour shall see His Birth.

Women, the fruit of your inner organs saw the light outside of you, but the Son of Man spreads his Light within and without.

Let us now live the Third hour, in order to understand it."

12

LA FLÈCHE

AFTER A LONG SILENCE

The "long silence" referred to in the title of this article was an eight-month hiatus in the publication of La Flèche. *As to the reason for it, we only know what Naglowska tells us. We do know, though, that she had material waiting to be published, including the two remaining installments of the serialization of* The Sacred Rite of Magical Love. *It is probable that she needed to find a new source of financial aid to help with the costs of publication. However that may be, publication resumed with No. 7 on November 15, 1931. The little newspaper was still eight pages long at this time, but they would eventually be able to expand it to sixteen pages, at least for a time (probably thanks to the sales of the books that she would add to her publication efforts). The resumption also coincided with the publication of* Magia Sexualis, *which must have brought her some revenue, as well as freeing her to focus on the newspaper again.*

Like the sea, Life sometimes becomes angry.

It seems, then, that the fragile ship that we are is destined to perish under the furious gales of adversity, under the hard and repeated shocks of the vengeful waves, which unknown forces direct against us . . . to punish us or to make us stronger?

Those of yesterday—the witnesses of the second phase of the historical triangle, which currently is tracing the beginning of the new line, the one that climbs and again sees the Origin—those of yesterday, we say, believed and still believe in divine punishment, inflicted by the Supreme Wisdom on individuals and on collectivities gone astray into sin, in order to bring them back to the path of Goodness.

Faced with calamities and evils of all sorts, they still preach, as they preached before, penitence and repentance. For, according to them, divine Mercy wishes the salvation of all.

But, oh sweet thing, oh consoling doctrine, none of the teachings remain standing, for the apostles of the New Religion are revealing the cruel truth, the truth of the Third Term of the Trinity, which bares the Knowledge of the Mother, while showing the sword of Her positive force. There is no penitence or repentance. A single thing exists: the imperial power of passive resistance to Evil.

To hold on, to hold on still, in spite of storm and tempest, to will, in the face of and against all, free passage through the personal will of the "I" of the Great Current of General Life, that, only, is what is right.

For the human being is nothing, and his conduct, good or bad, has no other value, in the eyes of the divine Lord, than the contribution that every act makes to the quality of good or bad conductor of the Universal Spiritual Fluid, to which we owe everything that has been given us: the flesh, because it is the root of the Spirit; the astral, because it is the accumulator and the recreator of the First Forms: intelligence, because it is the mirror of God.

The man who folds, suffocates with fear in the middle of the unchained sea, under the sky streaked with electric fires, under frozen rain and howling winds, the man who renounces his primordial dignity as a reorganizer of that which is into that which will be: this man will never know where the Polar virtues shine, where the new Strength of the Morning is born, and where the paths cross that lead from the earthly plain to the Mountain of Glory.

As much as the man crushed by evil may call for help, no pity will be shown him; for it matters little that the number of the good should be great.

It matters—at the terrible hour that now begins—that the triage of the material should be done.

The Third Temple must be built. Solid stones are needed, and precious metals, clear crystal. New materials are needed, tried by fire and purified in water and acids.

The Great Architect of the new construction no longer has time to wait for future generations. That is why He no longer cares about healing the sick or correcting perverse natures. From a teacher, He is becoming a *justifier,* and He is letting loose upon the earth the One who carries the name of blasphemer, in order to rapidly put to the test and choose that which will be useful to Him . . .

And Life becomes angry and takes on the aspect of the furious ocean.

Foamy waves, gray with rage, repeatedly throw themselves against the ships that we are.

Lightning streaks the sky, and men lose their reason. But it's not a matter of either punishment or correction. It's about a final test . . .

Immobilize your personal wills. Forget yourself completely—ah! can you?—and have only one desire: to understand the reason for all that.

It is necessary that the response to this question—the response that we have just formulated—should shine forth in you spontaneously.

It is necessary that the Voice should speak in you, that you yourself should become this Voice, indomitably.

For here is another atrocious thing: accepting our word does not suffice. We cannot save you, and what we say is nothing but a warning, a cry launched in the desert.

In the hour that we are now living, only prophets will pass the Threshold. The Ark of the Third Term only receives chiefs, creators, warriors without artificial weapons.

Everything that is putrefaction will die in putrefaction, and the pure will not be allowed to bring the impure with them.

Weakness is a sign of impurity. Be strong!

13

THE DOCTRINE
OF THE THIRD
TERM OF THE
TRINITY

The following articla appeared in La Flèche *No. 7, November 15, 1931. It is unsigned, but was clearly written by Naglowska.*

✦

The Divinity is triple: the Father, the Son, the Mother.

The Father is the beginning point of the fall, from the Origin toward the plane of division and multiplicity.

The Son is nostalgia and desire for universal redemption, combatted by the Adversary inherent to His nature: Satan.

The Mother is the return toward the Origin, after the definitive combat and the reconciliation *in the Son* of his two opposing natures: the Christic nature and the satanic nature.

The Son detaches himself from the Father and divides himself in two: He is double.

The Mother proceeds from the Father and from the Son, and contains both of them: She is triple.

Only the Father is homogeneous.

The three aspects of the Trinity—the Father, the Son, the Mother—are successive in time, but simultaneous in their Eternal Presence in the regions not involved with the plane of division and multiplicity.

The succession—Father, Son, Mother—is justified thus:

The Father is the Male principle, which accomplishes the act of the negation of the Unique Spirit; it is love oriented toward the flesh.

The Son is the principle of the second negation, that which in the flesh rejects the flesh; it is love oriented toward the unreal, the love of the infertile heart. The Son is neither Male nor Female: he is on this side of the two divine sexes. That is why he is beyond sexual beings.

The Mother is the reestablishment of the Male principle in the inverse sense: She affirms the Unique Spirit, and her love, starting from the flesh, is oriented toward spiritual realization. She consoles and glorifies the Son, for She makes his dream of sublime purity complete in multiple life. The Mother appeases the combat between Christ and Satan, leading these two contrary wills on the same path of unique ascension. The Mother proceeds from the Father and from the Son, and she is successive to them in the temporal subordination, because negation is not converted into affirmation except by means of negation.

When the work of the Mother is accomplished, that of the Father begins again, for the three aspects of the Divine Trinity repeat themselves endlessly.

In human history the three divine phases are reflected in the form of three types of religions, which constantly succeed each other, determining three types of civilizations, which we find in the cycle—or triangle—to which we belong in these three religious-civilizations: the Hebrew religion, the Christic religion, and the religion of the Third Term, which is being announced at present.

The symbol of the Hebraic religion—a Religion of the Father—is the rod hidden in the ark. Its ethic protects the reproduction of the species.

The symbol of the Christic religion—a Religion of the Son—is, on the one hand, the cross, and, on the other, the sword: the renunciation of the sexual act and scorn for life. But in the shadow of the Christ, the worshippers of Satan deify woman's womb in secret orgies, which maintain the dynamism of the march forward. The white Mass of the transsubstantiation is thus attenuated by the black Mass of the redynamization of the flesh, without which it would become anemic.

The symbol of the third religion—the Religion of the Mother—is the arrow launched toward the sky. The golden Mass, which it will establish, will glorify the real love of the flesh, in order to extract from the latter the renewing and ascendant spirit, which will make all things new upon the earth.

Blessed are those who shall assist at this Mass.

14

THE POLARIZATION OF THE SEXES AND THE HELL OF MODERN MORALS

This article is from La Flèche *No. 7, November 15, 1931, and it is signed "August Apôtre," one of Naglowska's pseudonyms.*

Men and women are essentially different from each other—and that is where we get the struggles and wars. The average man and woman will never understand on their own the reason and the details of their different formation—that is why peace cannot come from the crowd.

Everyone knows that on the physical plane—in the domain of the flesh—the man *gives* to the woman, who *takes*.

But one ignores—because official science doesn't admit it yet—that on the mental plane, that is to say in the spiritual domain, unexplored by discursive consciousness at our average degree of evolution, it is the woman who gives, while the man *receives*.

The man is the transmitter, the positive pole, on the physical plane: his flesh penetrates the flesh of his companion and leaves there the blood of fecundation—but in the spiritual shadows, there where the Unknown reigns, it is the woman, the positive mental pole, who pours out into the man, the negative pole, the fecundating spiritual seed.

It is this double operation that constitutes coitus, and woe to the man who receives an inferior gift while he sows the best of himself. The degeneration of the human race is caused by the *loss* that any degrading coitus represents in the cosmic economy.

The man cannot progress except by uniting himself *regularly* with a superior woman, and the woman cannot advance along the line of perfection if she does not receive the fecundating and illuminating sperm of the man frequently enough.

But the sperm of the man is weakened in its illuminating power each time that the spiritual compensation coming from the woman is insufficient, and, for its part, the invisible mental seed of the woman is dulled and made anemic, if the blood of the man brings her bad nourishment.

What we have just said is sufficient to explain the hell of modern morals.

The religions of the Father and of the Son that ruled the sexual relations of humankind—with a view to the healthy and *normal* birth of the child (the religion of the people of Israel)— but also with a view to the *sanctification,* that is to say to the interior awakening, of the virgin (the Catholic religion)—these true religions are from now on forgotten. We are now in the dark age that denies the preceding phases of the historical triangle, to open the door to the new phase: the phase of the religion of the Third Term of the Trinity, which we are announcing.

The dark era was predicted from the beginning of our centuries, and one knew from the beginning that *the Negator would be unchained and precipitated upon the earth in our time to accomplish his work of destruction.*

That had to be and that is, but it is painful for those who are living this hour, and men and women will suffer and sickness will consume their bodies for as long as the new truth is not proclaimed and accepted, reestablishing order in the wreckage left by disorder.

Humanity suffers and will suffer yet more, for jealousy devours it because of sexual chaos.

The man, unaware of his spiritual receptivity (because pride reigns in him), goes on the hunt for women, seeing only their bodies. If he is healthy and strong, he wants all of them, and is even jealous of other men acting normally. It's the first cause of war.

The man can love the flesh of all the women who are more or less pretty. The physical realm allows him this because it is just and noble to put oneself out for a great number. But the spirit forbids the male to adore more than one female. And because of that it is said that every (adulterous) sin will be forgiven a son of Israel except the sin (the adultery) against the spirit.

Man has the right to be polygamous according to the flesh, but he must be monogamous according to the Spirit.

The spiritual fluids are neutralized by their contrary natures, that is why the one who *receives* from all women keeps nothing from any of them; his worn-out flesh grows pale from it.

For the woman this truth presents itself in the inverse sense: it is the Spirit that permits her numerous loves, but it is the flesh that demands for her a single husband. That is why the breasts of Isis are multiple, but her receptive organ is single. That is also why the law of Israel, which was just, fixed every adulterous woman to the pillory.

But the dark era through which we are passing is unaware of all that. Women have declared that they consider themselves equal to men, and men have decreed that they are only flesh. It is the great scandal of our century, and the chaos of modern morals comes from it.

Humanity suffers from it, as the Just foresaw. The evils and sufferings of the human race will only pass when the religion of the

Third Term of the Trinity, the religion of the Queen-Mother, shall be imposed. In that blessed day the law of Moses will be put right for everything connected to marriage.

The law of the sanctification of virgins will be maintained for the education and preparation of priestesses, whose role will be, thereafter, to love ritually. Ritual love, this great operative mystery that will replace symbolic Masses, will spread the new healing grace over the whole of humanity.

15

PHARAONIC AND PHALLIC TRUTHS IN RANDOLPH

This article, which appeared in La Flèche *No. 8, December 15, 1931, was signed "M. de N."*

❧

Responding to a great number of requests sent to us by our readers, we publish below a chapter of Randolph's *Magia Sexualis*, which masterfully summarizes the great American's thought relative to the central problems of human life: the intimate relations of couples and their meaning in the grand scheme of social and world organization.

To please our friends, who are concerned to know the analogy that attaches the doctrine of *La Flèche* to that of P. B. Randolph, we include, after the chapter in question, a commentary by Maria de Naglowska.

Magia Sexualis, Chapter 4
The Magical Chain and the Divinities

The arcana dealt with in the preceding chapter are brought together under the title of *Mahi Caligna,* that is to say *the science of the ancient age,* because the generations that preceded us knew them and cultivated them.

We venture to affirm that because we ourselves have received them by *tradition,* and because we find testimonial to them in fabled monuments, erected in honor of the divinities of ancient Egypt, in the thrusting lines of the obelisks, which rise up to the blue sky like fecund phalli of the sandy flatlands.

This evidence teaches us that the sacred law of love rules not only the earth, but the whole universe.

We find it's revelation in Asia, in the sculpted images of divinities, whose arms, raised to heaven to bless or to terrify, attest to the truth of our doctrines and symbolize the power of the holy connections of love.

Besides, whatever one may say about it, the phallic truth is at the base of all the rituals of the secret societies, and the sacred art and the holy scriptures of all nations speak its mystery to those who know how to read them.

The hierophants of ancient Egypt knew the suggestive power of art, which is why they made it subservient to religion, imposing strictly determined laws and means of expression on the sculptors and painters.

It was a great benefit to humanity, for, impregnated with certain truths, thanks to the images and to the prayers, constantly seen and heard, the believers realized them automatically in their sexual couplings. And in this way, utilizing the creative energy of all the couples, the priests really populated the astral sphere with divinities and demiurges, nourished, in addition, by the vital power of the imagination of the masses. The people's astral group thus became powerful.

For love, divine force, endlessly creating, by the joining together of the positive and negative atoms, was nourished by the mystic exaltation or by the fright of the masses, prostrated before the altar; and the latter became, through the generations, the vase where the forces gathered, which brought, according to the will of the one commanding, good or ill, light or shadow, life or destruction.

Love is the only universal law, which rules the infinite spaces and deploys an irresistible action everywhere that life reigns, and a people among whom the nuptial practices are always in conformity with the eternal laws constitutes a great magical chain, binding the material sphere to the higher spheres.

From that there results an alliance of human forces with divine or spiritual forces, and the intelligence of Man then acquires the possibility of dominating both here and there. Mankind becomes the master of good and evil, and makes use of it according to his will.

This is the principle and the truth that, under such conditions as we shall establish here, makes enormous the responsibility of a head of state, who would be at the same time the supreme initiate and the religious chief of a people.

But, on the other hand, when religion is effaced and humanity forgets the primordial truths that we are reestablishing here, and gives itself blind shepherds, the evils that fall upon nations are greater still.

And when the anger accumulated in the higher spheres is unfurled upon the earth, because of the injustice and licentiousness of human life, no man has the power to stop the scourges and to master the storms that destroy the world.

These are the critical periods in the history of humanity, and each race has had its part in it.

The Commentary of La Flèche

We accept every word of what one has just read. We realize, as did P. B. Randolph, that evils accumulate on the earth when chaos reigns in the sexual practices of couples and when art and literary production go beyond the sacred laws, so well understood on the other hand in the strong periods of history.

And it is for this reason above all that we revolt again against the malevolent action of English Theosophy, which, while it has the key of truth, propagates a lie to more easily augment the number of its adherents.

The *truth* proves to us that every individual belongs totally and in all the manifestations of his life—even to the most intimate—to the collectivity, which, in its turn, is not right unless in all of its acts it is aiming for divine progress; that is to say, as we have already said on other occasions, the harmonious realization of the celestial rhythm, whose three stages carry successively these three symbolic and synthetic Names: the Father, the Son, the Mother. (See our summary of the Doctrine of the Third Term of the Trinity in issue seven of *La Flèche*.)

The lie that the ignorant support, excusable because of their spiritual blindness, and English Theosophy, inexcusable because the truth has been revealed to them, pretends, on the contrary, that progress is individual, thus encouraging the perturbing vanity and egotism . . .

No! Individual progress, "reward," and salvation do not exist, and no heroic act attracts any real benefit—that is to say spiritual—to him who does not work except for himself, without recognizing his close and obligatory solidarity with all. He who allows himself to be crucified—morally or materially—without making of it a collective offering; he who does not die for the resurrection of all, that one does not gain anything, either in this world or the other.

But when a single person truly makes the connection with the higher forces, the communion between heaven and earth is established and everybody profits from it: those who are aware and those who are not.

For such a connection automatically unleashes the pouring out over all of the divine energy, which, thus, is actually received by the whole of humanity. The tide does not ask whether the hollows of the bank desire its waters; it fills them because it encounters them.

But the obstructed channel remains dry. That is the case with the man who rebels. That is the unique freedom that is left to him, because rebellion is inherent to the nature of the Son (the Second Term of the Trinity). The rebellious man realizes the work of Satan, but—and we have already said it—this work is sometimes necessary.

Still, the intractable link putrifies and decomposes, for it soon lacks the regenerating force and sickness leads it to definitive death. The obstructing link always succumbs under the pressure of triumphant life; and rebellion, even the revolt that is necessary and foreseen in the divine drama, is always vanquished. Such is the satanic tragedy . . .

But to return to P. B. Randolph, we are happy that his work has finally appeared, for this book brings to humanity, in the dark hour in which it finds itself, the scientific light of which it has need to find the strength to bow before what is hidden and to accept the religion that we now announce to it.

Magia Sexualis brings positive proof of the great, primordial force of sex. This book scientifically demonstrates the truth summarized in the chapter that we have just read, namely that the intimate life of couples must correspond to the divine laws, not only for reasons of problematic hygiene, but above all because of the duty of each to live only for all, for only thus does one live for God.

To live for all does not mean to exercise charity. Giving is nothing, it is about being. He who perfects himself and at every moment conducts himself in conformity with supreme justice opens the gates that separate us from the divine. And a door opened by a single person remains so for all.

It is not necessary that each one should strive to become a great magician; passing others up is in no way useful. It is sufficient to love the one who goes before: his march is ours.

16

THE EXTINGUISHED
TORCH

This article by Naglowska appeared in La Flèche *No. 8, December 15, 1931. It was signed "Auguste Apôtre," (one of her many pseudonyms). It is interesting to note that Naglowska is not here advocating anything that she did not do herself: she went to the church of Notre Dame des Champs every afternoon to meditate.*

⚔

Interest in the "marvelous," in the exceptional, is, to be sure, quite widespread at the present time, but what isn't so much is the ability to understand things that are out of the ordinary.

Thus, one finds in all the halls of Paris, where conferences are given on occult problems or phenomena, a very numerous and always attentive public, but one realizes, when the audience asks questions of the presenter at the end of his discourse, or from the things that the audience members say to each other, that very few people truly realize what the point of occultism is, and still fewer the demands made by this subject on students and those proficient in mystery sciences.

Most often, seekers into the occult are only looking for a purely external instruction, that is to say intellectual, and they are far from knowing that the domain that is the subject of occult studies cannot be understood except on condition of a true awakening, in the human being, of an interior life developing beyond or at the edge of contingencies.

It is certain—and every reasonable being knows it—that one cannot assimilate a new notion unless one already has something in his memory that is analogous or similar. Our capacity for taking in knowledge is made in such a way that we cannot receive anything in a vacuum; we must first form the base—the *full liquid* as the sages say—upon which we will then fix the new ideas and realizations.

Now, the base is lacking for most of those who, in Paris, frequent the occultism courses: the basis of interior experience that places itself on the margin of daily life. Quite rare, indeed, are those among the inhabitants of the City of Light, the men and the women who live, independently of the facts and conditions of everyday life, a persistent and real dream, a dream peopled by other than what happens on the street and in the houses.

Modern man agitates himself too much, under the pretext that life is difficult, and he no longer even realizes that the more he agitates himself and the more he smothers the feeble spark of true life, without which he would be nothing, the less he can understand of the occult.

Man smothers the pale torch that, alone, would be able to illuminate him in the dark hall where he has engaged himself in coming to the world, and he is astonished that light is not given to him by someone else.

At the same time no human is unaware that it is not enough to interrogate the mirror, it is also necessary to illuminate it.

Certain of our readers ask us what to do to recognize the torch and how to make use of it to live a dream. Certainly, to answer that would be to open the Great Gate, because to understand that is to truly become initiated, it is to truly commence the slow march that infallibly leads to the foot of the Altar.

But that is where all the difficulty lies: it is impossible to live a dream while participating in human agitation, and, on the other hand, it is difficult not to succumb in the temporal struggle if one renounces the agitation before having discovered the torch: the weak spark of true life that shines in every person, for without that they would be nothing.

First, then, discover the torch: go every morning or every evening to a Christian church and immobilize yourself totally: don't watch anything that is going on around you, and force yourself to hear neither chant nor organ.

The ambience of a Christian church is propitious for the first meditations—complete immobilizations—of weak beings, that is to say those who are vigorously pulled along by the human stream.

The strong ones, that is those less engrossed by the cares of hard times, can try the same discipline in a café or other public place where a world thirsty for amusement is swarming. Meditation, or rather immobilization in a place of pleasure, triumphantly rekindles the interior flame.

But do not do that which is good for the strong if you are weak, and do not do that which is for the weak if you are strong. It will be of no use to you to fool yourself.

Do you still ask me how you will know whether the torch has been reawakened? Oh! Don't worry about that: if your life becomes animated, you will know it.

Go every morning or every evening to a Christian church: there is little chance that among you there are any strong ones.

Do not pray, do not think of anything earthly, and totally stop the chaotic game of your imagination.

Do not see anything, do not hear anything: do not fall asleep.

When you know how to be deaf and blind at will in a Christian church where mystery hovers, the torch placed within you, since you are alive, will illuminate you.

But it is possible that you may be very weak. It will then be necessary for you to take yourself to the church for a very long time, perhaps all your life, but do not be alarmed: in Christian churches there is that which the Second Term, the Son, has left to men: the possibility of profiting from the strength of the strong.

We shall speak of it again another time. But frequent the assemblies and conferences of the occult sciences just the same: the strength drawn from the church will be of help to you there.

17

THE INITIATIC COURSER AND THE FEARLESS HORSEMAN

This article was on the front page of La Flèche *No. 9, January 15, 1932, perhaps indicating the importance that Naglowska attached to it. It is obvious that she wrote it herself, though it is simply signed "La Flèche."*

❖

If the prophet, illuminated by celestial vision, giving him new life and strength, wished, in addressing himself to the masses, to tell them exactly what he had seen and understood, the people, terrified from his first word, would no doubt tear him apart, for he would be odious to them. The imperfect man fears celestial truth, because he senses in it an intransigent adversary.

This explains why the "envoys of Heaven"—the privileged ones who, after hard tests, have seen the cosmic Law and understood its glacial justice—hesitate to unveil the veritable drama of mankind's becoming divine.

Anxious, still, to offer the incorrigible cohort a comfortable trip across the river that separated the bank of the foolish from the holy island of Joy, they make an effort to throw bridges over the dangerous waves and seek to master the waters instead of mastering the people. The god of the waves becomes angry then and floods the riverbank and drowns the people.

For no one shall cross the river if he has not first conquered human nature. No one shall participate in the happiness of heaven, in eternal life, if while alive he has not broken the circle that imprisons him in the *human species,* if he has not broken the thread that attaches his life to that of the great collectivity, which does not permit him to take sublime flight.

But the secret is there: what must he conquer? What must he annihilate to acquire spiritual liberty? Is it the animal howling in the forest of various appetites that haunts the individual? Is it the desires, the needs of the flesh? Does the pale and anemic man, the weak man with his bones showing pass up the others? Does the isle of Joy want sick people? Some have said so, but they were wrong.

No, the animal is necessary. It constitutes the only element in the human species that is really divine, that is to say in conformity to the Will of Heaven. The animal desires what the divine Trinity wants. To understand that is to receive the first real initiation.

But after that it is a matter of learning something else, and it is there that the difficulties arise.

Indeed, the second initiation into the hermetic mysteries teaches us how to make use of the impetuous courser, which is only a means of setting out on the Great Road.

To stop at the first lesson is to decay, for to deify the animal is to fall lower than it. That is the first sin.

But to mount the divine courser, to adapt oneself to his wild gallop without losing one's reason and without falling off, to hold the reins with an expert hand—this is initiatic: *for the courser must lead us across the waters of the river of the separation to the second life.*

In vulgar terms that signifies that after having roused the flesh, we must draw from its deep inspiration until from our carnal love for the opposite sex the kiss of peace at last comes to us: penetration, through the opposite sex, into the region of divine glory.

But how to explain that to the foolish men and perverse women of this century? How to speak of these things to those who know only two alternatives, equally false: the return to unconscious bestiality (the first sin, which imprisons us in the human chain) or the anemia of the flesh, caused by the fear of the divine courser (the second sin, which condemns us to death)!

For the moment we will only give this one indication: to mount the divine courser (the natural desire of the flesh) means to voluntarily suppress the *need aroused,* in order to receive from it, in the course of special meditations supported by an appropriate diet, spiritual illuminations that will be nothing other than the humanly intelligible word of the divine spirit coming out of the beast.

But let us make no mistake. What has just been said equally condemns those who preach the holiness of virginity and the others, who support unrestrained license. We are, in putting forth our rules, as much against the white as against the black, for the white leads to an impasse, and the black into the chaos of degradation.

Man has in himself the sublime animal that has not forgotten the law of the Trinity that wishes the fall (First Term) and procreation. But the fearless horseman, formed by the second initiation, knows how to let himself be led by his superb mount to where the kiss confers the word of God (the Third Term).

He then receives the supreme illumination, which sheds light on the four cardinal mysteries: the mystery of birth, which is a person's entry into the closed circle of the human species; the mystery of the first marriage, which is the experiencing of the divine courser; the mystery of divorce, which is the victorious mounting of the beast; and, finally, the mystery of the second marriage, which is the entry into the Temple of God. That is where the acquisition of powers commences, which leads to immortality, that is to say to the breaking of the circle, which imprisons us in the nature of the human species.

From that moment, the initiate is a Freedman, a King, whom the people obey with ease. Power is given to him—for he has acquired it—to attract other humans into his new kingdom, others who do not have the strength to meet the challenge themselves. If necessary, a new Church is formed, a House, which offers salvation to all who enter it, full of faith, of love, and of hope.

A strength, more mysterious still, allows him to even attract people in spite of themselves. Those who experience this force, speak then of the charm of the free knight: they follow him without asking where he is going.

But the human *species* fears the Freedman, and seeks to prevent his formation by all means. This is natural, for the Victorious One is, indeed, the adversary of human stagnation.

18

THE INDIVIDUAL SOUL—DOES IT EXIST?

The following article appeared in La Flèche *No. 9, January 15, 1932. In it Naglowska took the risk of expressing ideas that would not please everyone even now and were probably less popular then. She signed the article with one of her favorite pseudonyms, "Auguste Apôtre."*

❧

Among the questions that have been sent to us lately, two, above all, deserve a conscientious response, for they translate the concern of every person who engages himself on the initiatic path.

They are the following two questions:

1. Does the doctrine of the Third Term of the Trinity, which we preach, affirm the survival of the human personality as an individual and conscious entity, evolving on other planes after death on the physical plane?

2. Do we affirm that it is possible for a person of flesh and bone to obtain positive proof of the Beyond by experience?

The article of *La Flèche* that one has just read already contains an answer to the first of these two questions.

There it is said, indeed, that Man must overcome human nature on this earth, by his own effort he must break the vicious circle that imprisons him in the human species, condemning him to eternal return. But, attaching itself above all to the problem of breaking the circle, *La Flèche* does not clarify what becomes of the imperfect soul residing outside of salvation.

Now, here is what the doctrine of the Third Term of the Trinity teaches us about this, the religion of the Mother, which emanates, while directing them onto a new line, from the two preceding religions of our triangle (see *La Flèche* No. 7: the summary of the doctrine of the Third Term of the Trinity): from the religion of the Father (the Hebraic religion) and from the religion of the Son (the Christian religion).

The personal soul has no survival as an individual and conscious entity, and it does not evolve on other planes, apart from a magical rebirth through the mystery of love on this earth.

This essential dogma separates us both from the Buddhistic inspirations and from a poorly understood Christianity.

The individual who is not regenerated while alive on the earth has no individual, conscious personality, for such a personality is of spiritual substance, and this latter is only acquired by the substantial transformation of sexual energy into spiritual energy.

In other words, we do not confirm the presence of an individual soul capable of evolving on other planes (or planets) except where there has been real victory of the fearless Horseman over the initiatic Courser.

All those who do not become initiated into this mystery through personal experience, as well as those humans left on the path, vanquished by the difficulties of the tests, stay merged in the collective soul of the species and fall again to the earth unendingly, without any progress or memory of the past.

On this point no reconciliation is possible between our doctrine and those of the Buddhists.

Pure Christianity, not weakened by oriental ideas, presents, on the other hand, an important point whose thesis we can take up without contradicting ourselves: it is the dogma of the salvation offered to mankind by the Christ.

For we say that the fearless horseman, after having conquered the beast, can include in his triumph all those who attach themselves to his steps.

This signifies that outside of the breaking of the vicious circle by his own initiatic effort, the imperfect man can be saved, that is to say carried beyond the species, if he abandons himself with all his heart, with all his intelligence, and with all his will to the one who has been able to triumph.

And furthermore: the Freedman of the waters can, if he wishes, save others in spite of themselves, by inundating them with his magical virtues. But the beings, snatched thus from the clutches of the species, remain, in the celestial regions, to the Victorious One who has brought them there, and on the higher planes they are his faithful servants and worshippers. So it is that the celestial armies are formed, which blindly obey their respective chiefs.

If a being, still stronger than was Jesus, could take from the earth all the energy imprisoned in the human species, the whole of humanity would fly off somewhere else, abandoning the earth to the plants and animals, which do not in any way fight the eternal rhythm of the Breath of Life. All of humanity would then go to build new dreams on new planets.

According to certain revelations, which it has been given to us to receive in the course of several magical contacts, we attest that since the time of the great Moses, humanity has tended, indeed, toward this fantastic goal.

It seems indeed that the Will, projected into the earthly world since the prodigious event of Mount Sinai, exerts itself to pull the totality of humans away from our planet. The realization of this Desire will obviously cause what one could call the end of the world, but we are told that this will not take place until the end of the third era of our triangle, which has just begun.

After what we have just told you, it is useless to separately answer the second of the two questions, which we listed at the beginning of this article.

Certainly it is possible for a person of bone and flesh to obtain positive proof of the Beyond through personal experience, but this proof is not such as the profane imagine.

Besides, how could it be otherwise: can I give an illiterate person a proof, sufficient for his ignorance, of the exactitude of an algebraic calculation?

It is the same with these truths: one cannot know them without having examined them thoroughly. And the first stage is certainly *education,* in the total sense of the word.

19

THE CARDINAL
MYSTERIES AND THE
GOLDEN MASS

The following article appeared in La Flèche *No. 10, February 15, 1932. It is obvious that Naglowska wrote it, but, as often, she simply signed it "La Flèche."*

⚜

Mystery is not the thing that one will never know; it is that which one does not know today.

Man can learn everything, if he truly perseveres, but most often he lacks perseverance, and he gives up, preferring the comfortable life.

He insults—to justify his laziness—all knowledge that is given only on the condition that one become wedded to it, sacrificing oneself, and he proclaims that there is nothing behind the sacred veil of the altar. Obviously, there is nothing for his fecklessness . . .

Today four principal *mysteries* limit, while troubling it, human life. They are: the mystery of birth, the mystery of marriage, the mystery of divorce, and the mystery of the second marriage. The individuals, men and women, who currently populate the earth—with some rare exceptions—know neither what these four things mean (these four cardinal points of the horizon that limit human vision), nor the path that one must take to know them. Today's men and women are blind, they do not admit the existence of the light, because it is uncomfortable for them to recognize that something larger than them moves them and penetrates them, and it is repugnant to them to understand that they themselves are only the very humble servants of this Great Thing that pushes them to act without their thinking about it, or knowing why.

Man no longer knows—though he has known it at other times!—that he is the slave of a divine force, that the Divinity itself does combat in him. It is because he no longer knows it, that he is incurable, that is to say doomed to death.

The combat of two divine forces, which goes on in the ignorant man throughout all his life, is what causes his death, for not having taken the part of one or the other of the two Adversaries, no Victory, no immortality, can be his. The force that animated him—*his life*—returns into the reservoir of the general force of the species, and begins a new effort elsewhere. But this is not a new incarnation of the same individual soul, as the orientalists believe, it is a new attempt, after recasting the ounce of metal poorly used into the large ingot.

The mystery of birth is the mystery of this new attempt. That is why, in the strong eras of history, when the Light of the Just shines on earth in the form of a true religion, recognized and respected, the parents joyously greet the appearance of the newborn, for they know that thus a new man comes into the world to defend the cause of the Just. . . . And the mother gives a name to her child to orient the Will that animates him toward a quality chosen by her.

Currently, ignorant humanity has lost the sense of the names. The baptism of the unaware little being, which should fortify him from the beginning of his trip on the earth, is now nothing but a sad comedy, for even the priests do not know their ministry. . . . Oh! it's not the fault of the wickedness of the people, it belongs to the times, to the inevitable night of time between two different days. Our century is that of the disappearance of the Light, and we live in the Shadow that prepares the new day. Happily the Dawn is near!

One will know soon, for it is thus that the New Lesson is presented, that the poorly born man can correct himself by marriage. *You cannot return to your mother's womb to come out again with another name, but you can again plunge into the woman who accepts you with love, to draw from her the Light that you are lacking.*

This is the second mystery that humanity will understand when the period of suffering, which begins now, shall have passed. The magical contact of purifying love will become again a wholesome rite, which will heal the individuals spared by the storm. One will then say, in presenting the young husband to the assembly of the pure: "Here is a new man among you."

But shameful debauchery will be forbidden, and every woman who does not wish to understand under what conditions love is holy will be banished from the renewed society.

Certainly all men and women will not be up to the strictest standards, but the inferiors will recognize the worth of the superiors and will thus benefit from their glory.

To the prideful ears of the perverse of today, what we are saying is a slap, but the Dawn takes no notice of the grimaces of fools, and the Sun pursues its ascending path in spite of the offense taken by the pale.

Do not ask us to tell you at this moment in what way marriage is holy. You will not understand it without a previous education of your body and your spirit. Besides, there is no use in getting ahead of the times. Today nothing is holy, because everything is unwell.

Today divorce is a senseless rupture, which prepares the way for another not less stupid. Today divorce has no goal of occult progress, that is why no one understands this formula: *divorce is the third mystery, whose exploration will be offered to people of the third era, when marriage has renewed them.* There is no need for virgins in the hierarchies, but for heroes voluntarily renouncing the pleasure that they know. And the hero does not leave the woman because he hates her, but, on the contrary, because he loves her. In the blessed days, which are coming, the mystical warrior will leave his hearth, his woman, and his child when the marriage has corrected in him all the bad orientations of his forces. Stronger than before, because more upright and better concentrated in himself, he will submit himself to the great test of the conscious and willing restraint of his primordial instinct.

Not all will be able to attain this height, and many men will have to stay at the level of marriage. But all will bow before him who is able and thus will participate in his glory. The admiration of the weak one for the strong is what binds him to the latter, it is the bridge by means of which the great one pours out upon the lesser the benefic fluid of his strength. It is not the strong one who gains when the weak one admires him, it is the lesser one who grows.

Today all of that is incomprehensible for the people of the crowd, but soon these principles will dominate customs. The suffering that is announced shall pass, and then the Great Word shall be understood. For the moment one pronounces it in a low voice and in the protective secrecy of the shadows.

Indeed, it is at midnight, at the darkest hour, that the first of the chosen (the men and women spared beforehand) shall soon celebrate the *Golden Mass,* that new and solemn rite that is the crowning of the "second marriage," the sanctification of love, whose value is collective and real in the sense that it symbolizes, by the true realization, the rose blossomed on the cross: sublime love realized for the redemption of all.

For the Golden Mass, which will unite seven men to three

women, duly purified of the vanity of personal appetites and chosen from among those rare ones who are not afraid when one says to them: *you will not eat and you will not drink until I come again*—will bring to the world the possibility of a new understanding, thanks to which the reconstruction of the human Temple will be able to commence.

The *Golden Mass* will sanctify the new marriage of the Just with Humanity, after the atrocious divorce of which we have been the victims.

20

THE GREAT DELIVERANCE

This very short article appeared in La Flèche *No. 10, February 15, 1932. Obviously written by Naglowska, it was signed with one of her pseudonyms, "Auguste Apôtre."*

❧❧

We are asked whether we are dogmatists or free-thinkers. It is, to say the least, a strange question, for from its first number *La Flèche* has proclaimed its faith in the most affirmative manner possible, in saying: the divine Breath has a three-beat rhythm . . .

We have never adopted the intellectual fashion that consists in leaving a thought that one has found fault with to evolve from there into a new conception. We have announced ours brutally, often without even worrying about the impression that would be made. We have tried to translate into comprehensible words and sentences (that is to say *French*) what has been revealed to us, and it doesn't bother us at all that many intellectuals don't understand us. We know that we will be understood later.

One will understand us, because soon the intellect will sleep among most individuals, and the subconscious, which our magical action nourishes now even where one does not read *La Flèche,* will shine forth spontaneously in their consciousness with our new doctrine. The inhabitants of the terrestrial globe will suddenly speak as we do, not knowing that we said it before they did.

The inhabitants of the earth will know all of a sudden that the Divinity that is triple, and one is not transcendent to Nature. They will know that in us God lives and struggles and pursues a determined goal; that the three aspects of the divine Trinity, Father, Son, and Mother, are successive in time and are repeated continually; that in human history, which is the mirror of the divine drama, there are strong and weak periods, of which the former are characterized by the victory of the corresponding religion, and the latter by their decadence.

Our period is a weak period, or nocturnal, because the religion of the Son is dead, while that of the Mother is not yet born.

The birth will soon take place, the day of the celebration of the first Golden Mass. This event will immediately follow the stormy period that is just beginning.

It is not a discourse that will triumph over ignorance, it is not a logical demonstration, but rather a sudden illumination of a great number. The fledgling leaves the egg when its life wishes it, and the woman gives her child to the world when the pains have been sufficient.

Humanity is suffering at this moment, but the great deliverance is near.

21

LA FLÈCHE

THE MAGIC SQUARE

*To the right of the title of this article, in parentheses, we find the
word "nouvelle," which can mean either a news item or a novel.
This was certainly intentional on Naglowska's part, leaving us
forever in doubt as to whether it really happened. Chances are very
good that it did, because Maurice Magre, writing as René Thimmy,
gave an account of what was probably the same event.[1] The article
was signed "Hanoum," one of Naglowska's pseudonyms.*

❧

Last year I made the acquaintance of a very strange woman. She
exuded an undeniable force of attraction around herself, and ignited
violent passions in those who approached her. At the same time,
nothing in particular stood out about this woman: neither wealth
nor beauty, nor extravagant attitudes. Her name was Vera Svetlan.
She had traveled a great deal, and spoke all sorts of languages. Her
French was impeccable.

A group of followers soon formed around this woman. I became
involved, and that is how I came to know all of them. Strange men
and women, to be sure.

One of them, for example, a tall and thin individual, with the mannerisms of an automaton and with a look that was always darkened by intellectual over-excitation, did not hesitate to prophesy, in his own name and in that of Vera Svetlan, an imminent new era that would necessarily be preceded by terrifying cataclysms. He even gave the exact date and place. Was he crazy? I don't know.

Another enthusiast of Vera Svetlan's group was serious. His long black hair advantageously framed his handsome face with its regular features. His gestures were those of a priest, and his gait, slowed by a war wound, was imposing. His friends gave him the title of Master, and surrounded him with a very marked respect.

Before commencing his discourse, the Master raised his right index finger and took on a mysterious air. "What I wish to say is not for you," his look seemed to say, and he continued in a low voice. "Isis, the Queen of the World, will incarnate soon. She will choose the body of a poor prostitute, a young woman condemned, humiliated, ill. She will come into this hall"—at this place in his discourse the Master wrapped the whole room in the café where we met every evening with a mysterious look, and, lowering his voice still more, he added: "She will come in the form of a ball of fire, spreading a strong odor of sulphur as she passes through. The ball will enter into the one chosen, and the poor girl will immediately be transformed: from sick and ugly, she will become beautiful and healthy; from scorned and humiliated—venerated and glorified. All those who shall have the good fortune to find themselves in this café on that day will have their part in the glory of Isis. . . . But there will be those who will be punished, my friends, some will be punished!"

Then the Master enumerated the various punishments reserved for the impious. It seemed that this man, with the air of a priest, took an evil pleasure in mentally torturing every woman and every man who in his eyes had been lacking in respect or admiration.

But the Master was not a bad person, I can attest to that.*

As tall as him and perhaps even more impressive was another friend of Vera Svetlan. He was called "Spring," no doubt because of his fresh and attractive mood, which sowed gaiety wherever he passed. He had a large face, square brow, the shoulders of an athlete, and harmonious gestures, full of natural elegance.

Why had he come into this group of crazies, where he maintained an attitude of benevolent criticism? Vera Svetlan said that he was her most precious friend and that her "work" would certainly fall apart if Spring left her. But why? No one ever explained that to me.†

Spring had many female admirers. One of them, an elderly actress in retirement, surely joined the Svetlana group only to contemplate him. It was a need with her, and a need that was also understandable, because in a few days Spring had made himself seem at least ten years younger.

The ex-actress was also an enterprising woman. It was she‡ who one day invited the whole group to experience Magic at her place. She tasked a young Spanish painter with the job of transforming her dining room into an "ardent chapel" for this occasion. The painter went to work with an enthusiasm worthy of his youth, and requisitioned from the studios of his comrades the lewdest and most *significant* things available. When one asked Vera if this decor, thus chosen, was

---

*[The description of the Master sounds very much like Henri Meslin, known to have been a member of Naglowska's magical group. The priest-like gestures, the seriousness, and the mention of the return of Isis, all fit Meslin, who was a gnostic bishop (Tau Harmonious), and wrote a book called *The Return of Isis,* under the name Frater Lotus. —*Trans.*]

†[There was one person in Naglowska's group whose name was the name of a season: Marc Hiver (hiver = winter). Marc Pluquet said that he was Naglowska's "friend," which suggests to me that they had a romantic relationship. He was a well-known art critic in Montparnasse, and may well have been the source of the money to publish *La Flèche.* This would explain the statement that Naglowska's work would fall apart without him. The mention of "benevolent criticism" is interesting too, since he was a critic by profession. —*Trans.*]

‡[This would be the hostess, "Gladys," of Thimmy/Magre's account. —*Trans.*]

really necessary, she answered: "He no doubt takes us for satanists." I must admit that this response seemed to me to be almost logical.*

The most beautiful woman of the Svetlan group, a vague American of oriental origin, always very elegant and exquisitely kind—perhaps the only one among these nuts who allowed herself the three regular bourgeois meals—was charged with sending out the invitations: little pink cards furnished with a charming quotation from Miss Dorville, the ex-actress.

We were on time at the rendezvous. The séance could begin at 10 o'clock.

We arranged nine cushions in a circle on the soft carpet, and each one took his place, legs ritually crossed.

Vera Svetlan sat in the place of honor, at her left the Master, at her right Spring. Beside Spring, of course, was the palpitating Dorville, and, next to her, the thin, exalted prophet. After the prophet came the beautiful American, the Spanish painter, and a couple about whom we have not yet spoken, but who merit being described in a few words. They were two strange creatures, always silent, endlessly hungry, and invariably entwined once they found themselves seated somewhere: in a café, if someone offered them a glass, on a bench on the boulevard, when the charitable heart was lacking: a man and a woman for whom death waited, two beings resolved to die together. Seated upon the bulky down of the hospitable Dorville, the man and the woman melted into each other and took no part in the "preliminary" conversation that began.

Spring was moved by it:

"Lovely Venus," he said to the elegant American, who really had that name, "how did you get the idea of inviting these two walking corpses to a séance for the formation of a magical chain?"

---

*[Many people still believe that Naglowska was a satanist, but it is a theory that has no congruence with her work, or with her own statements. She seems to have allowed, and even fostered, the misconception though, probably because it was good for attendance at her weekly conferences on the rue Vavin. —*Trans.*]

Venus did not have time to answer, for the Master had already raised his right index finger: "At any serious magical séance, Death must be present," he said, as always, almost murmuring. "These torches of life that are being extinguished elevate the importance of our reunion precisely by the putrefaction of the flesh that they represent. But, Dorville, just the same you should offer them something to reanimate themselves." "Indeed, what an unpardonable omission on my part," Dorville exclaimed, very happy to be able to move about and attract the attention of Spring to her beautiful legs in green silk stockings. "I have ten bottles of excellent bubbly. Spring, would you like to help me to serve our friends?"

Spring, too, wanted nothing more than to be able to move his muscles. He got up with a movement that was harmonious and full of grace. A few minutes later, everyone had a glass of bubbly in their hand, and we were waking up the entwined, moribund couple to make them drink. But they only accepted a single glass for the two of them.

The wine did everybody some good: the prophet became exalted, the Master prophesied, Spring cheered everyone up. Without protesting, the American accepted a tender caress from the Spanish painter.

During this time, Vera Svetlan, her glass of bubbly set on the carpet beside her, contemplated or dreamed or prayed.

The moribund couple were the first to notice the strange magnetic current that began to be set up: the man shuddered, and the woman was afraid, hiding it on the shoulder of her lover. The others became silent and exchanged astonished looks.

"Let's form the chain," said Vera Svetlan, "and with a common desire let's wish for the presence of the Guide among us. At this moment he is leaving the snowy crests of the Siberian mountains and he feels attracted to us."

Spring still had strength to resist the spell, and said in an ironic tone: "I greet the venerable Guide, but I wish to know his name."

"Spring, please be serious," the American said.

"We will baptize him ourselves," the Master whispered.

"The great Guide, who has left the Siberian mountains, is coming to us quickly," the sick woman suddenly mumbled, raising her pale, blond head above the shoulder of her friend. "It is because we're here, Marc and I, that he is coming here. It is our common Soul, our single soul, supported by two pitiful bodies that are ready to die, that attracts him here. Oh! I see him, he has frightening eyes."

Wobbling, weak on her legs, Martha got up like a ghost and went to the middle of the circle. She had on a long dress of very thin material. This dress, which was black, seemed red to all those present.

Marc looked at her as if what she was saying was perfectly natural. Everything about him was calm, he did not make the least movement.

"Have you put a spell on him?" Spring spoke into Vera Svetlan's ear, but she made a sign to him to be quiet.

"Listen to what she says," she said in a loud voice, addressing everyone.

"The great Guide doesn't have any need of the rest of you, of any of you gathered here. It is for us, for Marc and me, that he is coming here. I already feel in my legs the wind of his steps."

Marc did not move. His gaze was fixed on Martha, but he did not seem to be interested in her. He looked through her, farther, beyond, and seemed to penetrate into a region where things other than life were important.

The Master asked him what he saw, but Marc did not hear him.

"Leave him in peace," said Vera Svetlan. "His consciousness is not in him at this moment, it is in Martha, it is she who *knows* at this moment for the two of them. And try, everyone, to be a bit serious, because there is danger for the couple."

"The old one, who is coming from Siberia, does he want to harm these two unfortunate people? Why do you evoke someone who is malevolent?"

"I don't evoke anyone," Vera Svetlan said. "We all wished for the presence of the Guide, and this *presence* was formed."

The beautiful American was paying close attention. The red color that enveloped Martha intrigued her, and with her eyes she looked around for the electric lamp that must, she thought, necessarily be found in the hand of one or other of the guests. She had made up her mind, from the beginning of the séance, to discover all of the subterfuges employed. But the Master consciously held his palms pressed to his knees, well separated by the ritual crossing of the legs; he had nothing luminous on him. Vera Svetlan was not looking to fool anyone, it was obvious.

The jovial Spring could not be suspected, for, even more than Venus, he doubted and looked everywhere for concrete proof. The thin prophet was occupied with his neighbor, the palpitating Dorville, with the secret hope of stealing her away from Spring. It was his personal business, but in any case it removed him from any desire to actively get involved in the formation of any kind of occult presence. The Spanish painter, the big "baby" of the meeting, what could he do?

Venus was still reflecting, when Dorville let out a piercing shout: "Look, look, Svetlan, Martha is going crazy!"

Vera Svetlan got up with a bound. "Out of the way, all of you," she ordered, "go to the back of the room and stay calm. Don't make the least noise; I told you that there was danger."

Venus, the Spanish painter, the thin prophet, Spring, and Dorville went to sit on the big divan that occupied the back of the room. The two women huddled one against the other, and the men became entwined with them as they pressed around them. Spring lay full length upon the floor, in front of the divan.

No one spoke, for what was to be seen was completely new.

On the carpet, in the middle of the room, the Master and Marc remained immobile: two

Hindu Buddhas could not have been more placid. Vera Svetlan, standing, in front of Martha, resembled a wild-animal tamer, galvanizing a ghost. Martha, red and transparent, slowly brought her bare, thin arms up to her head.

Was Vera Svetlan commanding Martha's movements, or was she trying to moderate them? Later on, this was the subject of ardent disputes and violent quarrels, but while all this was going on, no one among the five spectators who had taken refuge in the back of the room could tell.

Still, Martha's hands stopped their slow ascension at the temples of her head, and her fingers appeared to sink themselves into her skull—so tight was their contact with the skin of her temples—and slowly, very slowly, because of the weight that they carried, Martha's arms took up again their movement of elevation, detaching her head from her neck, like a crown from one's hair.

When Martha's arms, puny and transparent, formed only a single column at a right angle to her body, we saw, between the raised head and the neck of the young woman, something like a luminous prolongation of the latter.

Vera Svetlan then, with a rhythmed step, approached the phantom-woman, extended her arms in a wide symbolic gesture, and slowly brought them together at the height of the luminous column that separated Martha's head from her neck.

Vera's hands crossed in the luminous column and came out of it, the right hand to the left, and the left hand to the right. This spectacle was terrifying, for at the precise moment when Vera's hands crossed in Martha's luminous neck, the latter's mouth let out an untranslatable moan, like the whistling of the wind in a chimney.

Vera Svetlan took a step backward and crossed her arms over her chest. Then Martha's head descended again to her neck and the luminous column fell to the ground, transformed into a ball.

Marc and the Master remained all the while immobile.

Vera Svetlan, after a short meditation, ordered Martha to pick up the ball with her hands. On the obeying palms of Martha it at once took on the expression and the features of a human head.

Martha presented this head to the audience, her arms held out in front of her, as one does in the Orient.

"Each one of you has the right to ask a single question, concerning the future. The head will answer," said Vera Svetlan, turning toward the five people who had followed this scene with bated breath; "Spring, begin."

Spring sat at the feet of the women, leaned his head against the knees of Dorville, and asked: "Will I find what I am looking for?" "No," answered the head.

"Your turn, Dorville," said Vera.

"I don't know what to ask," simpered the poor Dorville, terrified, "well, this: will I be happy?"

"No," was the response.

"Your turn, Prophet."

"Will I be healed?"

"No," the head said again.

"What must I do?" asked Venus.

"Love."

"And me?" mumbled the painter.

"Seek."

Spring was, to be sure, the least fearful of the group, but he, too, felt chills in his spine when the head, which had just pronounced the word "seek," suddenly took on the expression of one who is making an immense and painful effort.

Only Vera understood what the head wanted. Moving rapidly, she stripped off her jacket, her thick, woolen skirt, and her low shoes. She now had nothing on her but silk: a thin, white blouse, a pink culotte that hid half of her thighs, and long, flesh-colored stockings.

Vera got on her knees in front of Martha, who seemed to not see her. The luminous head, which had spoken and was now suffering, was thus exactly above Vera's head, and as the lights scattered through the room were deceptive, it seemed, from the divan, where the three men were grouped around the two anguished women, that at this moment Vera had two heads: one covered with thick hair, and the other, unreal, made of fire.

The ends of Martha's fingers, between the two heads formed six black points with a disturbing aspect.

Vera held her arms in front of her, meeting the hidden sex of Martha, and pronounced in a firm voice, repeating them three times, three syllables of an oriental language.

Martha then shuddered slightly and like a barely-animated doll, she spread her feet a little, in such a way as to leave a passage between her two legs.

Vera then slowly bowed to the ground. She extended herself flat on her stomach on the carpet and passed her head between the absolutely unfeeling feet of Martha. The nape of her neck was thus under Martha's sex, and the beginning of her thighs was beneath the luminous head, whose suffering continued.

This scene was suggestive. The two women, one petrified and standing, the other stretched out on the ground, formed a living square, whose volitional center immediately connected up with the exact place where the head was, supported by the rigid hands of Martha. Then, the suffering of the head ceased and a new look shone from its eyes. This was a real ray of something that individually struck the five persons huddled on the divan. This something *ignited* them, and there was, in the group, an immediate sexual transport that precipitated the men upon the women: three against two!

And while this was going on as we have described, Marc and the Master remained immobile at their first places behind Martha, who was unaffected by it all.

But when the five humans had accomplished, *because they could not do otherwise,* the habitual rite of terrestrial love, Marc called Martha, and she leaned back into the arms of her lover, while Vera, still prostrate on the ground, recited a new prayer.

No one had seen how the luminous head had disappeared.

22

THE PRIESTESSES OF THE FUTURE

This article appeared in La Flèche *No. 12, May 15, 1932. According to a note in a sidebar to the left of the article, the little newspaper had missed its previous publication date of April 15, due to financial difficulties. For the same reason, this issue was only four pages long, instead of the usual eight. This article was signed "Hanoum," one of Naglowska's pseudonyms.*

❧❧

One cannot know the Truth, the Law, the Justice, or the Intelligence that preside over the evolution and maintenance of the Universe, if one does not first climb the *Mountain* where the air is pure and where the divine Breath is not contaminated by the protestations of human egotism.

One will never know in what the transformation of sexual energy into spiritual energy consists, or how it operates, if one does not first remove himself from the vicious circle that imprisons the human species and keeps it on the *plains,* condemned to procreation.

One cannot learn these things from the mouth of the Freedman who has climbed the dangerous slope and triumphantly operated according to High Wisdom, because the new things that he knows in his new state are too different from the limited reality of those who only inhabit the earth.

An abyss separates the Courageous One from the lower region, and no one will triumphantly climb the dangerous slope without first having swum across the raging river that separates the *plains* from the *Mountain* . . .*

The law of life on the *plains* is based on individual egotism. On this earth, one works for himself or one succumbs.

But in the raging waters of the *river of separation,* it is a matter of losing the very notion of a personal self! It is about totally getting rid of everything that attaches us to ourselves (of everything that allows us to live on the *plains*) and then one of two things: either one arrives at the other bank, one recognizes oneself in the light of the universal Self, or one is lost to never find himself anywhere: neither on the *Mountain* nor on the *plains,* nor in the universal Self, nor in the individual Self.

That, then, is the definitive death, eternal slavery in Hell (in the elementary forces of the visible world), on the gate of which Dante wrote: "Leave all hope, you who enter."

For the river that one has to cross belongs to the Spirit of Evil, to the Destroyer Spirit that opposes the harmony of the visible creation.

Let us say this thing more frankly still: one does not cross the *river of separation,* which surrounds the luminous *Mountain* with a dark and restless wave, without the permission of Satan, the Adversary of the Creator, *who protests day and night against multiplicity and division and calls for the re-establishment of Unity within the Supreme Light.*

---

*[In Naglowska's symbolic language, the Mountain always represents the initiatic process. The plains, on the other hand, represent the mundane world inhabited by the uninitiated. —*Trans.*]

Satan is the force that one must evoke to break the fetter that limits us. . . . And the formula of evocation that is effective for this purpose is a formula of love!

How many mortals are capable of understanding that?

The man who evokes Satan to submit himself to this nocturnal force, or rather to subject it to his human will (to the will of his individual egotism), does not get from the Demon anything more than secondary powers, powers of sorcery, which are of no effectiveness for real transformation of the vital energy, for the victorious crossing of the black river.

To give oneself to sorcery is to aid Satan in his sterile rage within the human realm, for the miraculous forces that one obtains by these means increase the protestation, but do not contribute to a new creation. In passively obeying Satan one spreads over the *plains* the storm that rages in the *river,* but one does not climb the slope of the *Other Shore.*

If, on the other hand, one exerts oneself to subdue Satan, if one tries, as does the White Church, to paralyze his breath by systematically extinguishing the light that He ignites in human consciousnesses, the result is no better, for no one can annihilate what God himself permits: the will toward return to the Luminous Unity! God permits Satan to speak into the ear of Eve, for His wish is for His Son to return to Him.

But this *return* only works by means of complete love, that is to say by means of the complete fusion of Satan's force with the divine force that animates the animal flesh of Man. For the vicious circle of the species must be overcome even there where the energy of procreation lives.

Having bitten into the forbidden fruit, Adam spread illness and death through the earth, but, right away Eve gave him two sons. For a single one who shall die, two shall be condemned to live!

And a religion was given to mankind: the religion of the procreation of the species.

Centuries passed, and the earth was peopled with diverse races and innumerable crowds. But in the spirit of some, the hope of the *return* remained alive.

The Christ came at last upon the earth, bringing a new law to humans: love, which dissolves in the flesh the will to die in order to transform it into a will to live. "I have conquered death," Jesus of Nazareth said, "come with me to the Other Shore."

But the people—the numerous people—did not understand what the *new love* consisted in. They hushed up the rare ones who knew the secret, and proclaimed that the love taught by Jesus was the love that was useful to the species: charity toward one's neighbor.

The White Churches were organized in this ignorance . . .

But currently Satan is redoubling his vigor. His storm howls everywhere and the modern Eve again hears his voice.

Satan says to the chosen woman: you will absorb me, for you love me; you will help me to pass into the man, for you desire him to realize his union with me . . . you desire him to make of him a god.

Many women see that as through a veil . . . Some are conscious of it . . . Others, still less numerous, understand it totally.

Those are the future priestesses!

23

A MAGICAL SÉANCE

This piece appeared in La Flèche *No. 12, May 15, 1932. Naglowska signed it "Xenophonta and Maria." This gives us a hint that it was at least partly fiction, because Xenophonta, or Xenia, was the fictitious heroine of* The Sacred Rite of Magical Love, *and Naglowska's nom de plume in that book and her alter ego. Here we also meet fictitious personae corresponding to two other pseudonyms used by Naglowska, "Auguste Apôtre" and "Hanoum."*

⬥⬥⬥

May 1, 1932. The five current members of the Company of the Arrow met at twenty minutes to midnight on the sacred carpet that still takes the place of the future chapel.

Five low seats are prepared.

Auguste Apôtre, the venerable old man, installs himself in the place of honor, his back turned to the North.

To his left, at a distance of two meters, counted obliquely in the direction of the East, sits the dusky Hanoum, while the blond Arrow puts herself across from her, at the West.*

Exactly in front of the old man, at the Southern extremity of the carpet, are the two young twins, Xenophonta and Maria.

The five personages exchange the ritual greeting, lowering the forehead to the knees. They raise themselves immediately and breathe deeply: the young twins three times, the older sisters six times, Auguste Apôtre nine times.

The night is calm. No breeze comes through the open windows.

The little hall is illuminated by five oil lamps, placed respectively on raised bases behind each of the participants.

The walls are uniformly painted a light yellow, but the night turns them black. The unreal sea extends afar its dark, unequal sheets. One perceives a constellated sky.

Auguste Apôtre breaks the silence. He says: "It is twelve minutes to midnight. At two minutes after midnight we shall begin the work. Maria will ask the first question, determining the subject of the debates. Hanoum will answer, developing the subject. When she has finished, Xenophonta will ask the complementary questions, pointing out that which remains obscure to her in Hanoum's exposition. The response to these questions will be given by the Arrow, for it is from the West that analysis comes, and after the Arrow, Maria will again speak to tell us in what way this work has been beneficial to her. We shall then immediately perform the operation that is useful to the sending of our message into the profane world. . . . For now, let us use the eleven minutes that remain to us for the magical rite that concentrates the forces and orients the current."

Having said that, Auguste Apôtre raises his arms to heaven, offering his palms to the exterior fluids. The older sisters and the young

*[We see that Naglowska has given these characters the names that she ordinarily used as her own pseudonyms: Auguste Apôtre, Hanoum, Xenia/Xenophonta, and La Flèche. The addition of her real name, Maria, completes the total of five "persons," who in reality are all her. Naglowska did have a magical group, but the "staff" of her little newspaper was fictitious. —*Trans.*]

twins immediately imitate him. That lasts for the space of a minute, then, the ten arms are slowly lowered, to the right and to the left, until the right hand of one meets the left hand of another and vice-versa.

Auguste Apôtre is thus joined to the Arrow and to Hanoum. The Arrow takes in her right hand the left hand of Maria, and Hanoum receives in her left the right hand of Xenophonta. The twin seated to the East places her left palm upon the left knee of the one at the West, and the latter supports her right hand on the right knee of the former. The chain is formed. Then, the four women fix their gazes on the enormous forehead of Auguste Apôtre, who slowly lowers his eyelids. He receives the mute prayer of the women into the triangle of his forehead and interiorly evokes the source of the mysterious knowledge of the Cone.

"Amen," Maria says, and at the same moment the five heads present turn to the right, their eyes toward the East. Each participant immediately fixes their gaze on the nape of the neck of the one in front of them.

That lasts two minutes, and Xenophonta answers: *"Amen."*

The five heads again take their normal position, but all their gazes are brought to the center of the magical chain that has been formed.

The four sisters bring their arms back toward their knees and cross their fingers at the level of the navel, the elbows supported on the thighs.

They will remain thus until the end of the mental work of the séance.

Auguste Apôtre rests his palms on his knees, the fingers extending forward.

At two minutes after midnight, Maria asks her question. She says: "What is the meaning of the Paschal holy day, and why is it called 'the Pasches'* in the West?"

---

*[In French it is "les Pâques," the original "s" having been replaced by the circumflex accent. The French word is plural. The word in Hebrew is "pesach," usually translated into English as "Passover." —Trans.]

Hanoum nods her head slightly and responds:

"The word *Pasch* signifies *passage* . . . When Moses, glory be rendered to his Name, brought the chosen people grouped around him into the desert that separates Egypt, the land of suffering, from Palestine, land of the reward, the red waters had to be crossed . . . for emancipation from slavery is acquired at the cost of blood . . . The passage, that is to say the Pasch, was accomplished in the blood of mankind, for it is the blood that receives and spreads through the entire body the rhythm of the new life . . . At the time of Moses, the individuals who composed the chosen people did not yet have the strength necessary for the individual realization of the crossing of the bitter water, that is why the Jewish Pasch is a symbolic feast that promises but does not yet give the desired emancipation . . . But at Rome, in the catacombs, the *passage* from slavery in the flesh to liberation in the spirit was really accomplished, thanks to the new fluids spread over the earth by the dead Christ on the cross. Because of that Rome put this word in the plural: the Pasches . . . At present, few people know these things, because the Jewish Pasch and the Christian Pasches are like dry leaves where there is no longer any life . . . humans no longer know the rites without which the intellect cannot receive the divine light and understand the Truth . . . Man no longer sees anything except what he can touch; that is why life is leaving him rapidly and he goes about the earth like a walking cadaver . . . A new Pasch is needed to give him new strength. It is necessary to renew human forces by the establishment of a new religion that will make it possible for the best to modify the orientation of their vital energy: from low to high and no longer from high to low and toward mortal crystallization . . . The regeneration must begin with the women, for it is by them that the men will be lost or saved . . . One cannot accomplish the new Pasch without the new woman, that is why the Arrow is a woman . . . My sisters, an enormous task is incumbent upon us: the creation of the new woman . . . She will be neither a doctor nor a worldly person, nor a "career woman." She will be a priestess, whose role will be to celebrate the *Mass* with a new intention. The Golden Mass! The Mass of Truth! The Mass of the Renewal! Here, my sisters, is my first and last word: humanity needs a Conductress, equal in moral value to Moses. . . . It is only thus that the Fall can be transformed into ascension.

Hanoum fell silent and brought her gaze to Xenophonta who must, now, interrogate the Arrow. The young twin absorbed the fluid that Hanoum sent to her and turned her head in the direction of the Arrow. The latter continued to gaze at the center of the chain.

Xenophonta spoke thus:

"The exposition of our Sister Hanoum is luminous for me and for my twin sister Maria, who represents us in the profane world. But the occidental world is so made that it retains the words, but it does not conceive of their meaning. The occidental world lacks creative imagination, that is why it never thinks deeply, and it always stops at the surface of the ideas expressed. To renew the man of the Setting Sun, I believe we will need some oriental priestesses. It is on this point that I desire a response from our Sister the Arrow."

The Arrow turns her head toward Xenophonta and nods slightly. Xenophonta continues: "Another concern is coming to me. The West has based its civilization on the Christian principle of the democratic levelling of all before Christ, the only superior. . . . Those who people this country have forgotten God, but democracy remains: the criterion of the reasonable is sought here in the lowest intellectual ranks. . . . How, this being so, will it be possible to tell free men that one woman is a priestess and another is not? For if even one among them came to know the truth of what we are putting forth by his own intimate experience, he would not acknowledge it, because his neighbor would not agree with him. . . . The citizen of a free country waits to know the average opinion of all in order to know what he can accept. . . . I wish to know from our Sister the Arrow how we can cut through this problem."

The Arrow then begins speaking, and says this: "Young Xenophonta is right: words teach nothing to the occidental world, for men from here do not know the correspondence that binds the word to the force of which it is the expression. The understanding of the Occidentals stops at the words, at each word separately, because it immediately undergoes its influence, which evokes in him a passionate reaction . . . and passion obscures reason . . . to get past this, a whole education is needed. . . . We are already giving it, but we will give it still better when the Temple of the Third Term of the Trinity has been erected."

The Arrow fell silent, having ended her discourse, and the two twins bowed in a sign of their gratitude.

Auguste Apôtre then said, "Maria, young twin, the floor is yours to tell us how and in what this work has been useful to you."

Maria rises, takes the plate containing her lamp from the base placed behind her seat, and advances, her arms extended before her, toward the middle of the carpet.

She presents her lamp, one after the other, to Auguste Apôtre, to Hanoum, and to the Arrow, then, placing one knee on the ground, she places the plate holding the lamp at the place on the carpet that corresponds exactly to the center of the magical chain.

She then lowers herself over the lamp and surrounds the feeble flame with her two hands.

The flame immediately becomes larger.

Maria then returns to her place and, standing before the Assembly, she professes the following:

"Just as this flame has grown larger under the influence of your lights, O elder Sisters, O venerated Master, my understanding has grown in force and in radiant power on contact with your Knowledge. . . . I see more clearly the images that I only perceived before through a fog and I now possess a courage that I didn't have. . . . The task that is incumbent upon me in the profane world is made easier, thanks to you."

Maria bows deeply and again takes her seat as before: the fingers crossed at the level of the navel, the elbows resting on her thighs.

The five personages remain silent for four minutes . . .

This lapse of time having run out, Auguste Apôtre rises and invites the four women to do the same.

He gives the signal for the beginning of the magical operation that is propitious to the diffusion of the message of the Company of the Arrow into the world.

The message is formulated thus: *may men's passions be calmed, and may women receive into their respective wombs the new power of understanding.*

Auguste Apôtre is the first to pronounce this electrical telegram, making each syllable of it resound separately.

The four women repeat it after him three times, as a harmoniously rhythmed choir.

Auguste Apôtre then crouches down in the middle of the carpet and lifts Maria's lamp above his head.

Then the older Sisters and the young twins begin the rhythmic gestures that prepare the dance.

The dance of the four women is slow, and they often bend their heads back, while the point of their fingers touches the sacred carpet behind their heels. They then bend forward again and resume the cadenced step to the sound of an interior music.*

The Sisters are graceful and their bodies supple and agile.

The light tunic, their only garment, rises with the rapid movements of the legs and an enveloping aroma then spreads through the hall.

The sacred triangle emanates new forces. The venerable old man orients them toward the profane world, in order to fecundate with a new seed the earth redeemed by suffering.

This document has been drawn up and signed by the two young twins.

Xenophonta and *Maria*

---

*[This is the first description of the Water Dance, which later appears in Chapter 11 of *The Light of Sex. —Trans.*]

24

THOU SHALT NOT KILL

The point of this article is to be found rather at the end than at the beginning. It appeared in No. 12 of La Flèche, *and Maria de Naglowska signed it with her own name.*

❦

Last Saturday we went to a meeting of the Montparnasse Club (46, rue Vavin), which has been functioning regularly for about two months now, under the direction of Madame Barquisseau, whose eloquence and lively intelligence are indisputable.

We heard a report that had been put together by Miss Reine, a midwife who preaches the scientific limitation of births with a view to avoiding war. Having been called to the bedside of a young mother, Miss Reine could not be there to defend her thesis, and Madame Barquisseau pleaded her case. With supporting documents, the obliging attorney made us aware of new legislation that would consider abortion to be a normal and just thing!

The hall reacted, fortunately. There were some very animated debates, and several persons agreed with us that the moment has come to reanimate the religious ideal in humanity, for no longer hearing the divine Voice, mankind no longer knows what it is doing in life.

The individual who lacks mystical experience is like an animal that only knows its appetites. Indeed, Miss Reine does not hesitate to compare humans to animals and would like for them to be bred like the latter, and the young materialists who lined up on her side spoke only of the sharing of goods and of sensual pleasures. It is a sad humanity that no longer knows that in it the divine Breath seeks its harmonious realization . . .

We took part, after the meeting, in the conversation that was struck up around a table in a large Montparnasse café. We wanted to know why these people, who were inteligent, had such a great fear of the word *religion*.

We discovered, after an hour or two of discussion, that for these democratic militants religion meant tyranny. They get this impression from the fact that, through the course of history, the Papacy persecuted the Jews. These generous-hearted people are not materialists except to wipe out the ideas that, according to them, tend to separate Jews from Christians. Their implied reasoning comes down to this: let's forget Christianity, so that Jews and Christians can become brothers.

But look what is happening. While the Christians, habituated through the centuries to humility and to self-effacement, willingly hurry to the call of the destroyers and sincerely empty themselves of their spiritual content in the name of human brotherhood, the sons of Israel, brought up, on the contrary, in the spirit of the solidarity of their race, carry out this effacement only very superficially, keeping deep in their hearts a marked preference for Moses. I am sure, because I have had the proof of it many times, that a great number of our materialists would take instantaneously to the idea of religion if one proposed to them that the whole world be grouped around the Seal of Solomon.

This doesn't seem like such a bad idea anyway, since it is not incompatible with the doctrine of the Third Term of the Trinity, which we preach. We have said quite often, and we still repeat it in this issue, that the Europeans belong to the cycle of evolution whose first two stages were successively the Hebraic religion and the Christian religion. To be sure, in our civilization we have the heritage of certain types of paganism, such as those of the ancient Romans, the Celts, the Germanic and Slavic hords, but the Construction to which we belong is Judeo-Christian. Our mentality is Judaic and our heart is Christian. The divine Breath, launched into the world from Mount Sinai, first touched the Brain (the Jews), then the Heart (through the Christ); now it wishes to penetrate still lower: into the Sex.

Let me explain. In accepting the Law of Moses, the Hebrew people accepted into their brains the idea that the human collectivity is the House into which the All Powerful Creator descends to live. The people of Israel accepted the pact, the Testament, by which men recognize themselves as slaves of God (whose Name they shall not pronounce), and He, in return, blesses their generations and grants them the goods of this world.

The Christ, in extending this same idea to all of humanity, gave also a new law: you shall love each other, and thus you will no longer be the slaves, but the sons of God. For, in accepting the Law, of which the Christ did not modify a single syllable, not only with the brain, but also with the heart, the slaves became willing participators, that is to say *freedmen*. They obeyed because their heart desired it, out of love.

Now Jews and Christians must together take the third step. They must recognize that Humanity is the Bride of God, the great Widow whom the human brain and heart, because of their individualization, still deprive of the joys of the Wedding.

Jews and Christians must understand and recognize that before God individualization does not exist and that all are spiritually present in each.

When this shall be done, mankind will understand in what way the Golden Mass is the realization of the promises contained as well in the Judaic symbols as in the Christian Churches.

The Bridegroom is currently knocking at the door of the Bride. Let us allow Him to enter: let us thus realize the mystery of the Seal of Solomon, which is also that of the Bread dipped into the Wine.

25

OUR MAGNETIC
STRONGHOLDS

This article, from No. 13 of Naglowska's little newspaper, is simply signed "La Flèche," which was one of the pseudonyms that she used.

<hr />

Who is it that does not understand the doctrine of *La Flèche?*

First of all, there are those who are slaves to their senses.

They are attracted to women of egotistical sexuality, who draw out much, empty the man, and give him nothing or the least possible, to leave him wanting again.

These men, when they are intelligent and understand their status as prisoners, seek to escape the chains of the flesh and study the different doctrines of liberation offered today on the book market.

Quite easily they allow themselves to be caught in the nets of the systems based on Buddhism because this literature allows weak men to take fancy intellectual attitudes without great effort or real sacrifices.

These systems divide the human essence into several superimposed planes, said to be *of evolution,* and they are convenient in that they make it easy for a person of average culture who has more or less assimilated them to say (in conforming to them, apparently) things like "at certain hours of the day I live on my lower plane, and I visit my lovers; at other times I transport myself onto the spiritual planes, and I hate what only my body has loved."

Having said this, men of this type sincerely persuade themselves that they belong to the human elite that has the right to preach chastity to others without in any way practicing it themselves.

They generally show themselves to be very severe with regard to all carnal love, sensual or sexual, and they hate *La Flèche* with all their heart.

What shocks them in our doctrine is our fundamental dogma that condemns them without remission.

In effect—and we have just explained it again for the benefit of Mister Guénon—we insist on the truth that evolution is in sex and not at all outside of the latter.

He who wishes to follow us will not find among us any excuse for his debauchery, for his slavery in the arms of the unpurified woman.

If he wishes to come with us to the other shore, it is necessary for him to cross the river of separation, it is necessary for him to sincerely practice the preparatory ascesis to submit himself thereafter to the rites of the magical love that really transforms sexual energy into spiritual energy.

Intellectual knowledge of these things does not suffice among us for admission to the priesthood in the Temple of the Third Term of the Trinity. It is necessary to become a creator, a real revealer of new moral values, for only in that way do we recognize our apostles.

You can say what you like about oriental or occidental traditions teaching this or that—as long as we don't have proof—in a given individual of a spontaneous pouring forth of divine ideas, we will not believe in his superiority, even if he recites by heart all that has been written until now.

And even for the oldest symbols we require a new reading.

May those persons whom these lines touch recognize themselves and repent!

There is another category of people who fear *La Flèche*.

It is those who have a presentiment that our doctrine will cause a social transformation in the world that is dangerous to all false values.

These fearful people accuse us of satanism, of luciferianism, of black magic, and of still other things in order to distance as far as possible from *La Flèche* all the good elements likely to adhere to it.

These adversaries of *La Flèche* recruit, as well, in the ranks of official Catholicism as in certain masonic, protestant, or theosophical milieus, and one finds a good number of them among those Jews who do not stay in the House of Israel except to cunningly profit from it.

But none of these adversaries can do us any harm, for our fortress is not made of stone nor of any destructible material.

Our strongholds are arranged on the waters and on the land like magnetic sources that human weapons cannot harm, and the radiance that emanates from them acts independently of human will.

That is why we do not fear anyone.

26

THE DARK ERA
COMES TO AN END

This article appeared in La Flèche *No. 14, October 15, 1932. Naglowska signed it as "Hanoum," a pseudonym that she frequently used.*

The Dark Era is reaching its end. The coming year, 1933, will mark the exit of the human tide from the dark Vault under which we have grown pale in the course of these last centuries, deprived of Light, deprived of Comprehension.

A new faith will soon reanimate the world, bringing to it the health and understanding that it has lost, and a sincerely accepted religion will lead the storm-lashed river that we are on back to the luminous prairies whose memory is rare among the people of today.

For, just as we have said since 1930, the Light of the Third Term of the Trinity, the Light of the Mother-God, shines now in the world, and with its beneficial rays it is already illuminating the minds that are best prepared.

The mass of humans is still refractory to the New Word, but the hour of its Redemption will soon sound.

The hour of its Redemption? The hour of its healing, for rather than faulty or defective, humanity is ill.

Present-day humanity, born of the generations that grew up under the Vault, is anemic and weak: weak and fearful. That is normal for any organism that the Sun has not caressed.

The man of today, the modern man, does not dare to affirm himself as he is, because, while he crawled along under the Vault barely lighted by a few paltry rays articially borrowed from the true divine Light, his huge shadow, projected upon the walls that limited his freedom of action, terrified him and inspired in him a horror of himself.

Face to face with himself, the man of today thinks he sees a monster, a beast with a thousand different aspects, whose only desire is to devour him, he and his will to "do good."

He believes that this beast is pursuing him, lying in wait for him at every step, watching his smallest movements, defying him, and teasing him constantly: when he is trying to prove to others—and thus to himself—his superior intelligence that doesn't exist, when he obstinately tries to demonstrate the courage and generosity that he is lacking, and, above all, when he tries to make one believe—in order to believe it himself—that his flesh is able to experience, and cause to be experienced, unheard-of delights, making him the superior man that he isn't.

Modern man looks at himself in his shadow and with bitterness realizes his irremediable imperfection.

All his life is made false because of that.

He hates and envies those whom he might profitably have been able to love and venerate, if he were happy with himself. He forces himself to wear a lying mask, while using up the strength that he could more advantageously have used for himself and for human society, if it didn't seem necessary to him to be superior. He forbids himself to live normally in the intimate hours, for he has gotten the habit of seeing shame and an enemy in his body.

He tries to conquer the enemy, scorning it and covering it with sarcasm, but that doesn't work for him either, for the flesh takes its vengeance on the man who does not respect it.

To top off his misfortune, modern man has forgotten where his unhappiness comes from, his sickness, the false intonation of his life.

He believes that he lets himself be guided by his intellect, by his reason, nourished by profane science, and he does not see that at the bottom of his deepest conscience something else dictates his conduct, paralyzing him in his thought and in his actions.

This other thing is the ancient faith of his ancestors, which modern man seems to ignore, but which still remains within him, driven back and compressed into the darkest regions of his memory.

In earlier times, when this faith was alive, the man knew that throughout his life his duty was to gain Heaven. To perfect himself spiritually, always, unceasingly, which is what was imposed on him by the faith of the Second Term of the Trinity, the Christian faith for which terrestrial life was only a painful passage.

Through many generations, through the centuries, Man has become accustomed to considering himself as something to be scorned, something unworthy, especially with regard to the appetites of the flesh. This opinion of himself persists in him still today, but while formerly, when his faith was alive, his whole being was sustained and illumined by the vision and the hope of the future life, beyond the earth, beyond death, today the modern man, no longer having this source of comfort, aims to make of his sterile efforts a sort of surrogate of the heavenly Paradise: the state of relative superiority with respect to his contemporaries.

If modern Man could be definitively free of the ancient faith, which no longer enlightens because its hour has passed, he would be healed of his suffering and would again begin to live normally:

respecting those who are his superiors, being happy to be who he is, and letting his flesh live as it must.

But Man cannot abandon the old faith before he has received the new faith, for this is still true: humanity would cease if faith ceased. For faith, conscious or unconscious, is the link that attaches Man to God, and without God, Man dies, because God is Life and nothing lives without Him.

But the new faith is announced, and the old can now grant Man his freedom: freedom to pass into the New Era, with a tranquil look and a straight spine.

27

LET US MARCH
TOWARD THE LIGHT

The number of La Flèche *that contained this article, No. 15, February 15, 1933, had fourteen pages, instead of eight, which was the most common number. This indicates that Naglowska's finances had improved. For the first time the print is large, in a single column, with a lot of white space in the borders. The white space, though, suggests that Naglowska's energy may have been flagging. Just a few months earlier, she had published* The Light of Sex. *It was already evident in the last two issues of the newspaper that the notoriety she had gained was arousing jealousies and opposition within the occultist community. Naglowska signed this article as "Auguste Apôtre," one of her favorite pseudonyms.*

❧

When a great new idea is announced in the world, the men are jealous and the women get angry. It is because the Announcer must be tested, and there is no better test than resistance to hatred. The greatest fatigues come from combat against the blind rages of the indignant profane, and often the Announcer begs the Force that guides him to spare him the bitter cup of abuse. But the will of the Force that has made its choice and selected him, remains unshakeable, and the Announcer gets up again and continues to carry his cross. . . . It is thus that *La Flèche* today takes up again its interrupted task . . . in spite of anger and hatred.

It proclaims, as it has before, and it will again, that the Second Era is expired, and that the Third Era, that of the Divine Mother, is beginning . . . at the midnight of our time, at the dark epoch of our multiple sicknesses.

La Flèche will not form any pacts—because this is forbidden to it—with the numerous small and fallacious lights of the night, with the stars whose tracks are comfortably traced in the dark firmament, those little stars whose pale glow does not bother the weakened eyes of men. *La Flèche* has received the order to project into the world the dazzling rays of the great Dark Force, which, in this tragic moment when all is platitude and incomprehension, obeys only God, protesting against the foolish exuberance of the sons of Man (*Satan*), who no longer know where truth is.

Men, until midnight of our time, have continued the life of the preceding day and thus have disturbed the regularity of the necessary reconstruction of the Triangle, which is not accomplished except by redirecting it into the obscurity of the new ascensional path of the new day. The sons of Man, who imagine that the Second Era still continues, oppose, without knowing it, the divine Law that does not tolerate the precipitation into the infinite of any of its three faces destined to repeat themselves successively, always according to the same procession: first the face of the Father (religion of the judaic type), then the face of the Son (religion of the Christian type), and finally the face of the Mother, after which the same things begin again . . . under other skies, at other hours.

The Adversary, the somber Satan, has the duty of speaking and acting each time that one Era finishes and a new Era begins. For the sons of Man are degenerating at this time, and their lamps have no more oil . . . If they did still have any, and continued to, the old day would be precipitated into infinity, and this would have been a disobedience. Now the disobedience of the sons of Man causes the wrath of Satan, who, in mowing down the evil sown by the impious, makes straight the ways of God. The triangle then regains its just form, because the angle is re-formed by the merit of the Adversary who mows down the evil sown by the impious sons of Man.

It is thus that at the present hour of our multiple maladies Satan is the only faithful friend of the immense Creative Force spread through the Universe. He is the Reason that emits its *veto* against the old day, which tries to persist in spite of the night, in spite of the new dawn. He straightens the ways of God, imposing on men the review of all values: that of "goodness," which is nothing more, at the present time, than a craven hypocrisy; that of "charity," which is no more than an offensive alms-giving; that of "justice," which has become an infamy mixing that which is unworthy with that which is noble; that of "pity," which is a blasphemy, and that of "prayer," *which no longer signifies anything but a little fear and sheepish habit.*

The Adversary, the great Satan, speaking to men by means of new mouths, will teach the humanity that still remains standing after the present storm the Truth of the Third Term. *La Flèche,* the organ of His magical action, will serve him as it has promised, to the end.

28

WHERE IS
SALVATION?

This is another article from La Flèche *No. 15. Naglowska signed this one as "Hanoum."*

※

What will you do to be saved, my unquiet disciple?

The first rule is the following: you shall not dream of your salvation, because if you dream of it, you will be worried, and the principal condition for the reawakening in you of the sacred fire, which alone can burn up your native naughtiness, is interior calm, indifference to your own tomorrow, material and moral.

To be just, that is to say to live in conformity to the great Universal Laws, the individual must harmonize himself on the terrestrial (practical) plane with the society that surrounds him, disturbing nothing, not overturning anything that exists, and above all not wishing for anything more than what the circumstances of life offer him. In this way his spirit and his intelligence are not monopolized by useless cares, and he finds time for wholesome meditation.

Wholesome meditation is that which has for its object not oneself, but the Universe, not the welfare of all, but the Laws that govern the world.

The individual who remains indifferent to what goes on in the exterior and does not worry about the advantages that he does or does not acquire interiorly, little by little hears the voice of the Universal Soul, the voice of the sublime Cone that whispers in his ear what is just and true. That is when his salvation starts . . . without his knowing it, in the shadows. For then, having reestablished contact with the celestial voices, the individual no longer has any trouble being just, living in harmony with what exists, and attaching his thought to the supreme things of the Spirit. . . . For, if you have enjoyed the music of heaven, that of the earth no longer charms you.

Consequently, oh disciple, here is what you will do: you will create indifference in yourself and you will wait. But I warn you: it is quite difficult!

29

THE KEY OF
SAINT PETER

The following article is from La Flèche *No. 16, March 15, 1933.
Naglowska signed it "Auguste Apôtre," a pseudonym that she used
for many of the themes that were closest to her heart.*

❈

In our nocturnal epoch of hatred and pride, one often abuses the
word "love," because, tired of suffering, tired of undergoing the injustice of the powerful of this world, the crowds voluntarily flock to any
place where this word is pronounced. And when the crowd is large,
the person who has attracted it takes in plenty. . . . The crowd is
blind, it does not reason. The words that strike its imagination agree-
ably immediately give rise to joy and fellow-feeling in its heart, and it
then pays for the pleasure provided. It goes back home happy. . . .
Should we blame those who thus take in what they need to live and
to bring prosperity to their various enterprises: the "free" and "popular" forums, the spiritualist newspapers, the various "studies," the
"philosophical" academies, the five o'clock teas, the paid banquets,

the vacation camps, the vegetarian and teetotaler restaurants? Must one reproach them for speaking of Love, with a view to provoking the generosity of the audience? Isn't that a human thing, very human, too human? And does any harm come of it? No, without a doubt. Exteriorly and for the people themselves, no harm results from this market in the word "love." Neither those who have pronounced it, nor those who have heard it change in any way after these meetings, and each one lives as before, in the same atmosphere of hatred and vengeance . . . For also, when one speaks of Love in our epoch of shadows, one generally hears only Charity, and when one says to the crowds: "Love one another," all one hears is "Support one another materially," which is not at all the same thing. . . . One entrenches oneself behind Jesus, who, it would seem, was the first to pronounce this formula. But what do we know about what Jesus meant when he said that? Who would dare to claim that he knows what Jesus really taught to his intimate disciples, to those who came to see him by night "from fear of compromising themselves in the eyes of the doctors of the law?" During those long nocturnal hours, what was the argument of him of whom Pilate said: "Behold a man," and whose contemporaries sent him to death because he called himself the "King of the Jews." Who will dare to say that he knows what Jesus taught to Nicodemus? . . . Love one another was no doubt a formula for the crowd, and the latter, through the centuries, has well shown how it understood it: "Give me what you have, and be happy that you are charitable." Today, as two thousand years ago, the understanding of this formula has not varied, and it will not vary, as long as one has not understood what Love means . . . Love, Love, the name of Rome, R-O-M-A. . . . Will one go to the Vatican to seek out the key of this mystery? Will one take up the book of the great Dante? *The Divine Comedy,* God's drama, will anyone wish to know it? No, because one wishes that God should be perfect, absolute, merciful, and above all generous. One wants Him to practice the famous formula according to which Love is lowered to the cheap level of Charity. One wants the grace of God for the pleasure, for the well-being of humans, and for that reason one will not understand that *God needs* people, needs their Love—carnal, sentimental, and mental—to reestablish His plan in the universe, His way, His will, endlessly combated by the Adversary, the somber Satan, who cannot do otherwise as long as the perfect couple does not exist and does not realize His redemption by means of the forbidden fruit, consumed according to the great Art . . . Satan, in the man, but through the woman, must come to love God, that is the supreme secret of Love, for the letters of the word indicate respectively: R the king (*roi*), O the equal and the eternal, M the mother, and A the new or renewed man. Omega and Alpha, the last and the first, the fallen and the pardoned, the renewed through the Mother/Lover. Then the King, the true man, becomes worthy of reordering the earth and all that lives in the Universe, because the two Equals, the Black and the White, then sign their Peace, the peace of their Love that neutralizes their hatreds One in the Other. . . . This will be the work of a man and a woman, who will form the first perfect couple on the earth. At each beginning of a third term of the Triangle, such a perfect couple is found. Today, one does not yet see them, because the New Religion has not yet united humans, by means of the New Faith, in a single vibrating and creative mental sheaf. . . . Today, rare are the men who understand these things, and the women, rarer still. That is why the Golden Mass, which is the true Wedding, the Wedding of redemption, cannot yet be celebrated, and Satan cannot reconcile himself with God, the Creator of the Visible World, who nailed him to the Cross of Shame, to impede his action. . . . And this was wise and prudent, for as long as the Golden Mass cannot be celebrated in all solemnity and before a large, respectful, and understanding public, Satan unchained cannot sow anything but death since his Communion with Life has not yet been realized.

. . . We, the members of the Confraternity of the Golden Arrow, wish for and prepare for this event. For here is the truth: it is first necessary to imagine the new men, and then to make them present by means of the Art; only after that, those who are incapable will be changed. . . . We do not call disciples to us, we create them. First in the idea, then in the image, later in reality. . . . May those who have ears hear us.

30

MASCULINE SATANISM, FEMININE SATANISM

This article is especially interesting, because it gives us some clues as to what Naglowska meant by Satanism (not at all what we would mean by it). It was published in La Flèche *No. 16, March 15, 1933. Naglowska signed it with her own name.*

People ask me if I present myself before the public as a disciple of P. B. Randolph, the celebrated American author of *Magia Sexualis*. Several serious occultists do. Here is my precise answer to this question: No, I am not a disciple of Randolph, for I am announcing a new religion in the world, whose revelation was given to me (not by a human mouth, nor by books) at Rome, at the exact moment when the cardinals meeting at the Vatican received from the *Celestial Messenger* the inspiration for the election of the present Pope. I've already recounted that in one of the numbers of the earlier series of *La Flèche*. This revelation, which I translated into human words in my recent volume *La Lumière du Sexe,* is not formally in contradiction with certain principles and procedures revealed in *Magia Sexualis,* but the light that guides me is not that which guided Randolph. I ask my contradictors to please remember this point, because its importance is enormous. While Randolph, still bathing himself in Hindu idolatry, believes, as theosophists of all nuances do, in the independent and individual life and evolution of each soul particle—a concept that leads in the last analysis to dreadful reinforcement of the spiritual egotism of men and women—I rise up with all my energy, because such is the divine teaching that has been given to me, against this disastrous idea, erroneous and generatrix of all the evils of humankind. I say, and I ask that one take note, that nothing is personal or individual, *either on earth, or in the heavens, or in the waters under the earth* (may those who have ears hear!). I say: nothing is in opposite to me, and I am not opposite to anything, or anyone, and among you who read me, no one is opposite to anything, or to anybody separate from you, and no thing, no being, celestial or terrestrial is opposite to you. We are not going toward Unity, we are Unity and have been since the beginning, which never happened. The idea of the separation of the self-styled particles of the Universe is an illusion of masculin satanism, and P. B. Randolph, just as all theosophists, all Catholic theologians, all Jewish rabbis, and all educated people in general, supports, as is just, a kind of masculine satanism. The head of the male, Reason, belongs to Satan, as we have said. It is masculine satanism that pushes away direct divine revelation and passes through the sieve of negating examination every truth spontaneously shining forth from the life force. Masculine satanism creates separation because it is separation, but its creation is fallacious. It is the No that opposes the Yes, and it dies without ceasing, for it is deprived of life. Meanwhile it is necessary, for it is the ferment that hosts life and without the struggle Life would not be. Since the beginning, which never was, the Elohim, the Yes and the No, have opposed Heaven to the Earth, confirming thus the principle of contrasts, which is the essential and profound basis of what is, of the Unique, which is and which we are. Until the end, which will never come, the Elohim, the Yes and the No, will continue their great solitary combat, their universal combat, which is translated everywhere and which forms everything. Consequently, error will subsist and illusion and death will not cease. Masculine satanism is immortal. It is immortal in the heavens, it is immortal on earth, it is immortal in the waters, under the earth. If the death that it generates stopped, Life would cease. Now Life cannot die. And because Life is, Death persists. Open your ears, serious and puffed-up-with-pride occultists, and try to understand this truth . . .

But in Satan there is also the feminine side. This is quiet most of the time, because since the Beginning words have been taken away from it. Sometimes God lets it speak, but only at the times when the suffering becomes too great, and then it is the song of the Swan. A time finishes then, and another time begins, just because feminine satanism has expressed itself. Feminine satanism is the principle of the new Birth, and its cry of joy announces the new Day. The Word is born then in the chaste womb of the woman; it rises to her head and speaks through her mouth, determining the beginning of a new Era. Feminine satanism generally keeps quiet, because it is the Guardian of the Threshold, the silent Guardian that opposes the solar phallus to prevent fecundation. It is its assignment to oppose fertilization, the joy of the Sun, because without this opposition, Life would not be. But when the suffering becomes too great and the test is too widespread, bending bodies that are too weak, the Guardian of the Threshold, Woman-Satan, Divine-Mother-Satan, pronounces her word. Then everything changes in the heavens and on the earth and in the waters under the earth, and during a sublime instant, the separation no longer exists, the man and the woman are not more than a single thing, the two contraries are dissolved into a single One, the cry of joy resounds, salvation arrives and Life triumphs.

We know that the following promise has been given to the Just: *the woman will crush the head of the malefic Serpent at the appointed hour.* Now, this is what I do. I crush the head of the Serpent, masculine satanism, and I proclaim the triumph of the Solar Shaft in the mouth of feminine satanism. There you have the difference between my teaching and that of Randolph, all of the theosophists, all of the theologians, and all of the rabbis. I proclaim the triumph of Life, because of the joy of the Guardian of the Threshold. This joy is spiritual, for it comes from the transformation of the waters of hell into the streams of heaven.

And now, may the learned director of *L'Astrosophie* of Carthage reread me. May the venerable bishop of the Gnostic Church at Lyon, who asks if my teaching is traditional, reread me. May the occultist-booksellers who refuse my book in their shops, reread me. May the shameless sexologists, who preach the dissoluteness of women, repent. May the doctors who understand nothing about it, but who engage in sexual philosophy just the same, blush in shame, for they are committing the sin against the Spirit, the only one which will not be pardoned, for they prevent all understanding of truth and cast humankind into mortal debauchery. They would do well to be silent, for Truth shines forth and will confound them soon . . .

Today is the brief instant of the triumph of Truth. Hasten if you wish to enjoy it. When the instant has passed, the lie will return, the lie of the comments. Then it will be too late. The elect, those who will have merited it, will enter into the new Temple, and the others will be crushed under the ruins of the collapsed houses.

31

OPEN LETTER
TO PIUS XI

This "open letter" appeared on the front page of La Flèche *No. 19, March 15, 1934. Its placement on the front page was perhaps indicative of the importance that Naglowska attached to it. Naglowska signed it with her own name.*

❧❦

The Pope of the Critical Hour

You have said, Sovereign Pontiff, that Christianity itself is threatened with death in this terrible time when nothing is still standing: neither faith, nor hope, nor even charity. The peoples detest one another, men tear each other apart, and women no longer know what chastity is.

Everyone wants only one thing: easy pleasure, fast, stunning. They look for that because they no longer have anything in their soul, and their spirit is empty, because it finds nothing.

For a long time now humans have said to themselves, "Let's not trust in anything except ourselves, let's not believe in anything except visible matter and reason, which invented mathematics; let us chase Christ from our hearts and let's proclaim openly that God does not exist; in this way we'll be free, and we'll freely exploit nature, enriching ourselves."

A hundred and fifty years have sufficed for this materialism to bear fruit, and you are touched by it yourself, Sovereign Pontiff. Interiorly, mankind has become exterior, and the Church, of which you are the head, has followed in this movement. Night is in men, it is true, but it is also at the Vatican and even, alas, in your spirit.

Will you tell me that I am fooling myself when I say that nothing scares you as much as true faith in a woman whose spirit is not asleep? Isn't mysticism what you fear above all? You demand blind submission from your flock, because you don't believe that one can, in opening the inner eyes, see something in your Church, on your altars, in your doctrine.

Yes, Sovereign Pontiff, the crisis of the present hour is there: in the nothingness of your Church and the nullity of your faith. Nothing but ineffectual words come out of the Vatican at the present time, because they are not sincere. Even more than in the masses, Christ is dead in you.

This has been fatal, and you know it as well as I do. You are not unintelligent in the profane sense of the word, and you have understood, since the beginning of your reign, that Christianity can no longer be pulled out of the swamp in which it is stuck without a new Word, the Word of the Third Term of the Trinity, the profound truth of which you know as well as I do. You know that this Word was given to the world at the precise moment of your election by the Conclave, meeting in Rome, after the death of your predecessor.

You know, that if you announced it yourself to the nations listening to you, humanity would be spared many evils. Humanity, having touched the bottom of the abyss, is ready now to begin the ascension. But you prefer to keep it on the exterior precipice, because you are lacking faith in your own strength. You hope that, for better or worse, the world will stay as it is until the time of your own end.

This is criminal, Sovereign Pontiff, and it is quite doubtful that you will not be punished for it. The forces, still impalpable, of the new Renaissance are pressing in invisible crowds around your walls. The resistance that you show them exasperates them, and if it keeps on, the clash will be furious. After the unhappiness of the crowds, it is your unhappiness that they are preparing.

For you have two choices: either you will light the torch of the Third Term of the Trinity under your dome, recognizing that love is not forbidden, but that it must be made sublime, or the love that you chase away will turn against you, as a savage passion.

The chief of the Italians, Benito Mussolini, has declared that the new generations need a mystique. He proposes to them that of distant voyages and sporting wars.

Aren't you in a position to tell him that this is still only a derivative, an external consolation, when the sickness is inside of people?

This sickness is called the absence of love, and it consumes men, because women, no longer having religion, no longer know how to love.

All is false in our nocturnal epoch, whose only spiritual light is the vague memory of an expired ideal.

Have the courage to reveal the new truth, find the strength to say that man and woman are created for each other, and that in the love of the two is hidden all Mystery, all Wisdom, and all Mystique.

Allow us at last to understand Dante and Beatrice, without looking for noon at two o'clock.

I have dedicated to you, Sovereign Pontiff, my volume entitled *The Hanging Mystery*.

My wish is that you may deeply understand its form and contents.

32

LA FLÈCHE

SAVING DISCIPLINE

This article appeared in La Flèche *No. 19, March 15, 1934. This appears to be the last time that Naglowska had much energy for writing in her little newspaper, which would have only one more issue, in January of 1935. Issue No. 19 contained advertising for her book* The Hanging Mystery, *which had just come out. It seems safe to say that Naglowska's health was already in decline.*

❧❦

Man wishes to be free. It is thus that he conceives of his happiness.

But society must limit him in every way, for, it is only at this cost that it can cause order to reign among the crowds and obtain an efficacious result for its many and various efforts, joined into a harmonious whole.

The more men are evolved (the older they are), the less painfully they bend themselves to the severe law of discipline, for on the one hand they understand the deep sense of the collective work and the relative insignificance of isolated individual work, and, on the other, having widened their interior horizons, they are driven by less violent appetites.

The superior man accepts the law without rebelling, the inferior man undergoes it with distaste.

But the superior man is rare, and the others are innumerable; because of that constraints exist, and slavery, draped in various disguises, will last until the day when a means shall be found to open everyone's interior eye, which permits one to see the Universe as it really is.

Opening this eye is the task of religions. Science adds to Man's knowledge, but it does not widen his capacities. It does not enrich him in his interior possibilities. It leaves him as he is and in doing so ensures his failure.

For to not grow interiorly is equivalent to dying and to rapid rotting.

Science enriches Man exteriorly, but it impoverishes him within himself.

But religion augments people.

By its hierarchical organization . . . for there is no true religion without its pyramidal social organization . . . it places the persons of proven value in the superior ranks of the human collectivity, in such a way that the ones below, seeing the light of those above, receive it effectively, thanks to the magical virtue of the admiration that real perfection gives rise to in those who have not attained it.

Exterior brightness provokes jealousy and base envy. True interior light emits rays whose charm is fecund, undeniable, and uncontested. One accepts it without humiliation, because it does not humiliate. It enriches him who accepts it and creates in him new possibilities.

The man on the bottom looks to the man at the top with confidence and hope, and the latter gives to him the vital force that he is lacking. Then the human cone is formed and the Divine Cone becomes wedded to it as the hair on a head. From above to below Wisdom then descends, while from below to above the Work rises . . . the work of cerebral thought, the work of the heart, the work of the sex . . . the construction of human arms.

But retain this: no one shall build the human cone on the debris of the current destruction, if it has not been given to him from on high to do this, if God himself (Life) does not speak fully through his mouth.

The human brain, whatever its force, will never know, if the divine Sun should not inspire it, in what manner to act, nor how to place upon the ruins of the collapsed building . . . the structure of the Roman Church . . . the foundation stones of the new construction: for without the help of the Sun the brain will never understand that the first requirement is the faith that animates and envisions and then the struggle for the realization at any cost.

The realization of what?

The realization of freedom in slavery, of interior liberty in rigorous exterior discipline.

"The Spirit breathes in you because it is free; but you will regulate each of your acts in conformity with the general Law, because you belong to all."

The Great Moses had said: "Be ye the slaves of God; it is thus that ye shall become the masters of this world."*

Later, Christ proclaimed: "Renounce yourselves completely and so ye shall gain heavenly joy."†

Today, the Invisible says: "May the brain of Man accept slavery, for it has no other destiny; may his heart love the Universe and God, his life, for it is his only plenitude; may his sex realize its magic, for victory passes under the Arch, but the Arch symbolizes the Yoke if it is not that of the Triumph."

The new building of the human cone must begin with sex, because before ordering the new hierarchies, capable of reestablishing order among the crowds and of judiciously harmonizing the common work, the men and the women must purify the root themselves, the feminine and masculine sexes.

---

*[This has a scriptural ring to it, but I have not been able to find it anywhere. —*Trans.*]

†[I have not been able to locate any corresponding canonical passage. —*Trans.*]

Now, no purification is possible in darkness and disorder.

O! Blind and deaf slaves, who do not hear the Voice of the Invisible!

You will curse the Eternal, if the joyous feast of the Golden Mass takes place without you, but you will not put yourselves on the way to get there in time!

You call for the chaotic liberty of the wild animal, and you do not understand that Man's privilege is precisely discipline!

The entry door to the City of free citizens is small and narrow. One enters by bending the spine. But on the public square the Arch of Triumph is taller than all the houses, and the freed warrior comes there on horseback, for his intrepid courser has been mastered.*

The intrepid courser symbolizes sex, and discipline must begin there, at the root of the human being. The man who is undisciplined in his sex is no more than an animal and all his pretensions are ridiculous.

The freed warrior is, on the other hand, a disciplined man who has understood the benefits of slavery. He guards his rank in the initiatic hierarchy, he obeys his chiefs without arguing, and passes the orders to the inferiors with no explanation.

But the wild, irremediable question "why?"—what is that about?

Do you want to remain savages and participate in the inevitable regression through the degradations of the lower animal species? Do you want the fall into the shadows, from whence the return is slow and painful?

A choice is offered to you: to obey or not. But if you do not obey, your loss is irremediable.

We have just begun the new line of the Triangle, the line of the Ascension.

All those who stay behind, all those who do not wish to accept the obligatory saving discipline are, by this very fact, thrown into the exterior shadows. The joy of the Golden Mass will not be for them!

---

*[This "courser" always represents human sexuality, which needs to be mastered and directed. —*Trans.*]

33

INITIATIC EROTICISM

This article appeared on the front page of the very last issue, La Flèche *No. 20, January 15, 1935. Naglowska signed it using her favorite pseudonym, "Auguste Apôtre."*

No one shall have a share in the joys and in the balance of the era of the Third Term of the Trinity, unless he resolutely engages himself with the path of Initiatic Eroticism.

The men and women who shall remain fouled in the shadows of sex, where the man loses his reason and the woman the freshness of her primordial intelligence, will be thrown from the triumphal chariot that carries only the chosen toward the Sun and glory.

Those who shall be rejected will form, behind the procession of the glorious, a lamentable train of individuals without liberty.

For this is true: only the victorious Freedman is free, that is to say the Disciple who has been able to conquer his wild mount to make of it a courser that is bold and obedient at the same time.

In traditional initiations, Man's sexual appetite is first referred to as a wild horse, and later as a war courser.

The wild horse carries the man who sits astride it into the laby-rinth of chaotic paths. It does not measure its strength, and it gallops randomly without reason or goal.

As long as Humanity found itself in its first hours, after the ini-tial fall, which was produced at the beginning of our Triangle, it was not possible to ask of the men of the crowd that they understand the necessity of mastering the "courser." It is certainly because of that that Moses, in forming the people of Israel (the people of *"him who has fought with God,"* and God is in the "courser"), forbid them all penetra-tion into the mysteries of Isis, which, at this period of Egyptian deca-dence, were nothing more than an orgy and a redoubtable perversion.

Reason had foundered in the Egyptian plague, and the first duty of Moses was to set it right in men.

To restore erring reason, sex had to be veiled and its function limited to the duty of procreation.

The law given by Moses was in conformity with this truth, and the people of Israel, who accepted it and obeyed it, relighted the torch of Reason on the earth, which cannot go out again until the end of our centuries of the fifth historical Triangle.

But, at the end of the first era, there was a new event. A spiritual Revolution, caused by the life and the passion of the Christ.

This life and this passion of the Man whose Reason was com-plete, lighted the torch of the Heart in Humanity. And Man was ashamed of his flesh, and he fought it to render it amorphous.

The Second Era began then, the era of the struggle, the era of atrocious tribulations. Nineteen centuries of sufferings, nineteen cen-turies of foolish chimeras, such is the bill that we sign today.

But, these sufferings were useful to us. They prepared in us, they accomplished in us, the transmutation of savage instinct into aspira-tion of a spiritual order.

The brutal love of the first era became, in the best truly and in the others conceptually, the subtle adoration of that which the flesh contains: the soul, some say; Life, answer the others.

The adoration of the flesh purifies the flesh, because wishing for perfection, it creates it.

What is purified flesh? It is the creative aerodynamization of a density that is too heavy.

Brutal love densifies the flesh and because of that obscures the Reason and the Heart. But adoration volatilizes what is opaque and remakes of Man what he should be: a Creator.

Now, adoration leads to eroticism, and replaces with the latter the simplistic practices of brutal love.

Eroticism leads to the Third Era, the one that lights in humans the torch or the light of sex.

But the touchstone is there: no one will accomplish an erotic work if he is not really adored by a woman, and no one will be adored by a woman if his game of love is not a poem.

It is therefor necessary that the man and the woman should be of superior essence for there to be eroticism.

The inferiors can imitate the superiors, but, not knowing how to create, their work is not worth anything: it does not lead the flesh beyond itself, and fortifies neither the heart nor the reason.

That is why it is just to say that the love of the vulgar is an abomination.

But what to say to him or her who asks himself how, from abominable, to became perfect?

Alas, there is only one answer. It is very simple, but infinitely difficult to apply: perfect the reason and the will that depends on it, then repeat, during a period that is more or less long according to the individual, the asceticism of the second era, and finally find the woman who is worthy of the sacred work and provoke in her the flame of love necessary to the re-creation of the man in his three principal centers: the center of the Reason, that of the Heart, and that of Sex.

But how shall I tell Dante where his Beatrice is?

If you do not find her yourself, no one will point her out to you.

And would you like your task to be easy? If so, I am sorry for you.

PART III
social questions

❧❦❧

Maria de Naglowska, who spent most of her life working as a journalist, was fully capable of writing about things other than religion and spirituality. In the later years of her life, though, we find that her religion and her spirituality colored everything else, giving her a paticular viewpoint as a social critic. Here, in Part III of our anthology, she writes about her own social thesis, about bolshevism, and about feminism.

34

OUR SOCIAL THESIS

This article appeared in La Flèche *No. 1, October 15, 1930. Naglowska signed it with one of her favorite pseudonyms, "Auguste Apôtre."*

In our days, an occultist publication cannot fail to take a position in the domain of the great general ideas concerning the reorganization of social regimes. It's not that such a duty is imposed on us by the public, which in any case cares little about occult action, hardly knowing the profound reality of it, but it is the stage where *magic operating in the world* currently finds itself that demands that each one that becomes a leading organ pose and respond to these questions: Is modern life healthy or unhealthy? Does it represent progress or a retrogression? If it is sick, where is the remedy?

We owe the uninitiated reader some clarifications, for we cannot assume that each will interpret the phrase "magic operating in the world" in the way that we do ourselves. Here, then, is what we understand by it:

Magic is the *science-life-action* that accomplishes, in a manner

that is undecipherable by ordinary understanding, a given and continued work, whose definitive end cannot be expressed in current
terms, for it is just there that the word of Christ is verified: "Do not
cast your pearls before swine, that they not turn against you and
destroy both your pearls and you."* For the rest, the definitive goal
of magical action does not directly concern humankind and its well-
being, for Man, his joys, and his sorrows are nothing more than quite
insignificant dust in comparison to eternity and the Great Unknown
that rules the universe—it is perhaps this that explains and in a way
perhaps even justifies the indifference in His sight of mortals in
general—but, nevertheless and however it may seem, humanity is
effectively a collaborator in the magical Work, and whether it wishes
it or not, it is above all through humanity that the Unknown acts
and brings about on the earth.

One of the principal tasks of *La Flèche* will be to make these
primordial truths known and recognized, but for the moment, we
shall content ourselves with only stating some points that are directly
connected to the thesis at hand.

There was a time, and history has kept its memory, when civilized humans, that is to say organized and disciplined, presented
themselves as a pyramid composed of four castes that were quite
distinct and superimposed one upon the other. At the bottom there
were the people devoted to manual works and to all practical needs.
Their fate was deplorable, and their characteristic was lamentation,
but they obeyed the *law of life* and that was the essential thing. Over
these people and living from their labor, there were the businessmen
and merchants of all kinds. They generally had material wealth, but
discontent was rife, for egotism does not give happiness. Still, they
were useful, because "waste needs sewers." Higher still, the civilized
human pyramid was comprised of the nobles or warriors whose joy
was combat and whose goal was victory. Those people had within

*Matthew 7:6

them the beginning of spiritual life, because their appetites were not only material. They often had less wealth than the merchants, but their heart drove them elsewhere. The highest caste, in this distant time, was represented by the teachers and masters of religion—the terms varied according to the races and nations—and these people who were relatively few in number were the true directors of the social life of the time. They accomplished their task as directors according to the wisdom that was vested in them, and what they did was good, because the Light was in them. The culminating point of the Pyramid was formed by the sacred King, neither clergy nor lay, whose justice was real because it was divine. Through the human pyramid, the hidden magical action of the Unknown was spread and worked in the world.

But the Unknown has an Enemy. It is the symbolic Serpent that wishes that each individual should go through the complete evolutionary cycle alone and arrive by his own merit (*isolated*) at the summit of the world's edifice. Speaking to Man the language that is to him the most comprehensible, he incites him to revolt against the pyramidal organization of society by means of the unchaining of the physical appetites. Where does this force come from, and where is it going? We will speak of it in our next article, which will be titled *The Symbolic Serpent.** Here, we give our general thesis without too many details.

The symbolic Serpent—we shall not give it any other name at the moment—has slowly but victoriously fought with the Unknown, throughout modern times. What happened with it in still earlier times does not concern us here. Early on it filled the kings with pride, then the religious masters, then the warriors and merchants, and finally, the masses of working people. The picture that humanity presents now is the perfect result of its work. The Light no longer exists anywhere, that is to say in any specified human category,

---

*[Naglowska does not appear to have ever written such an article. —*Trans.*]

and if a few weak voices arise here and there to remind one of the Sun and indicate its orientation, they are certainly neither listened to nor respected by the crowds. The unleashing of passions is general, the anarchy of customs complete. To extricate itself from the darkness where it is about to capsize, humanity has today a single lantern of which it is very proud: science. The latter alleviates its misery a bit, vaguely cures it of some physical pains, reduces its expenditure of muscular energy in the conversion to machines, but gouges the real wound: pride. Worse still: it makes the veil lowered over the eyes of Man thicker and thicker, to prevent him from seeing clearly and from knowing what the *miracle* is. . . . Your smile, reader, confirms this truth.

Now, where is magical solar action in all of that? Is it vanquished, dead? Has it abdicated?

That is the true subject of our present discourse. The social problem only interests us as in relation to this question. Would re-establishing the pyramid, as some suggest, smooth the ways of the Unknown and remove the shadow for the triumph of the light? Scorning the present status and returning to an old regime?

No, categorically no, for that would be a foolish work, accomplished by fools. It would be theater, without the divine comedy. And, besides, humanity can do nothing in the catastrophe from which it suffers. When a serious doctor proposes to cure a sick person, he studies his case, analyzes to the extent that he can, the set of contrary forces that struggle for or against the illness, and attempts, within the scope of his weak means, to strengthen the good against the bad. That is all that Man can do, the rest does not depend on him.

In the defeat of the Unknown and the victory of the symbolic Serpent, those who feel within themselves the reawakening of truth can do only, according to us, one useful thing: identify themselves, as much as possible, with the essence of the Light and thus become again its active rays. The selection of those who are strongest spiritually will then happen by itself and the hierarchy of real values will be reestablished as a consequence. The one who shall effectively be the king, that is to say the true summit of the human mass, will of necessity receive the solemn anointing, and each one will voluntarily obey his word, because what he will say will be just. But human revolutions and reorganizations under current spiritual conditions are all equally senseless.

Our position with regard to the social problem is then, definitively, the following: we abstain from taking part in human struggles having material aims, but we hold that what is happening today before our eyes is anarchy and barbarity. It is the agony of the Pyramid whose stones are now all on the ground. But since it is foolish to dream of the reconstruction as long as the night is dark, we will only do one thing: with all the strength of our interior will, we shall call the Light-Spirit of which we wish to be the conducting cables. We hope actively, that is *magically,* that by the force of our energy, offered voluntarily and consciously to the Great Unknown, the latter will shine again through us and will put an end to the destructive work of today. We shall say to him "come," until such time as He shall come. . . .

But magically hoping does not mean crossing one's arms and passively awaiting the good time. On the contrary, the *good time,* the *new era,* the *rebirth of the light on the earth,* must be *our creation.*

The difficult point is exactly that: to act personally and willingly without care for one's own person, for one's own appetites, to go beyond oneself while at the same time remaining essentially oneself. The individual will must decentralize itself, stretch itself, so to speak, to become the axis, while ceasing to be the center of one's own movement. Be your pivot, don't be your center of gravitation—that is the formula that we propose. Straighten yourself, become stiff as an arrow, it is thus that you will launch yourself in the right direction, carrying along those who are like you. A great effort is necessary and patient teaching to arrive at this realization; we wish that *La Flèche* may obtain this success.

35

IS BOLSHEVISM COMPATIBLE WITH THE DOCTRINE OF THE THIRD TERM OF THE TRINITY?

Naglowska wrote this article as part of a piece called "Les Questions Sociales," in La Flèche *No. 15, February 15, 1933. The rest of the piece was on feminism, and appears in the next chapter. Naglowska signed both parts with her real name.*

⊰⊱

On all sides people ask us if bolshevism is compatible with the doctrine of the Third Term of the Trinity. We are eager to respond to this question, especially since it sometimes causes trouble in some of the milieux that are sympathetic to us. Here is what we can say in this regard:

If the bolshevik doctrine presented itself simply as a method for practical organization of the distribution of earthly goods, there would be nothing there to criticize from the point of view of the metaphysic that we preach, for it is perfectly indifferent to us whether the means of production and the production itself should be recognized as private or collective property. What is important is order in human affairs, and if the order is better obtained in one way than another, it is obvious that we should choose the one that is best.

But, unfortunately, bolshevism does not present itself—at least not up until now—as a simple practical doctrine; it encroaches upon a domain that does not belong to it, and that is where the question becomes serious.

Indeed, since their establishment as an official political party at the beginning of the twentieth century, the Russian bolsheviks have clearly pronounced themselves in favor of the materialist philosophy and have systematically given themselves to combating even the idea of any and all religion, qualifying the latter as "bourgeois." The bolsheviks straightforwardly say that "all religion is a perfidious invention aiming at the oppression of the working class, consequently, the proletariat must fight fiercely and with perseverance against the mystical, against all religious orientation of the spirit."

Logical in that amongst themselves, the bolsheviks turn their weapons generally against all spiritual philosophies, thus obliging anyone desirous of living in peace with them to consider the problem of one's daily bread as superseding all the rest. There, obviously, we will never follow them, for us the first rule is the exact opposite: the question of the daily bread should be the last thing that preoccupies every just man, every man and every woman desirous of knowing Truth. In that, also, we are in agreement with all sincere representatives of all the religions of the past and of the future.

We counsel our disciples to reduce their material needs as much as possible, in order to increase their free time, which, according to us, should be devoted to the study of things of the Spirit and to wholesome meditation. According to the state of spirit of the bolsheviks, it is, on the contrary, necessary to attach oneself as much as possible to material things, to visible wealth, and work collectively to acquire it night and day, if necessary. The abyss between the bolshevik conception and ours is, consequently, manifest.

But that is not all. What also bothers us about the bolsheviks is their total incomprehension of the sexual problem, which they pose in the most absurd way, namely: as a question of "the right to pleasure."

We have said and repeated in all the numbers of our first series of *La Flèche* that superior sexual love is a priesthood, and inferior sexual love is the duty to procreate. Love practiced for pleasure is a scandal, an infamy!

The bolsheviks, who will never understand that the spirit is in the flesh and that sacerdotal coitus awakens it and carries it to the top of the head, thus causing it to shine forth upon what is commonly called the consciousness, will never be in agreement with us when we repeat that there is no salvation for the world and the generations other than in sex, and that the night that still weighs us down will not be driven away as long as the Light of Sex is not recognized, at least by the elites. Humanity will continue in its error and will adore the Golden Calf, in the capitalist or communist form, as long as the Temple of the religion of the Third Term of the Trinity, the temple of the Divine Mother, is not erected. And wars will rage, revolutions will break out, women will sell their flesh, and men will lose themselves in vice and other debaucheries, as long as the Truth that we proclaim is not understood.

But after that, it will matter little how humans choose to share their earthly goods. Truth will be there, shining forth in the new Temple of the magically united couple, and men and women will know, for one will tell them, and they will understand it, how they must live. All this will happen in its time, at the predetermined hour. In a year? In fifty years? Tomorrow? It matters little. Everything happens in its time.

36

LA FLÈCHE

THE NEW fEMINISM

This article and the one in the previous chapter were published together in a piece called "Les Questions Sociales," in La Flèche *No. 15, February 15, 1933. Naglowska signed them with her real name.*

※

I read with great interest the excellent article of Colonel Alexis Métois* in *La Griffe*. Indeed, the doctrine of the Third Term of the Trinity (the Divine Mother) may well give feminism a new orientation, in the sense indicated by Colonel Métois, if the movement replaces women's political ambitions, fighting for a better destiny for humanity, with aims that are more natural and at the same time more spiritual: those of the priesthood.

Women must indeed, and very soon, replace men in the higher direction of public affairs, but not by the parliamentary path whose inherent errors Colonel Métois so correctly points out, but by becoming high priestesses of the Temple of the Third

---

*[Colonel Alexis Métois was a French military man and writer. He must have had an interest in new religions, because he later became a supporter of the Caodai religion of Vietnam. The director of *La Griffe*, Jean Laffray, also came to be associated with Caodai. —*Trans.*]

Term, from whence truth and wisdom will at last shine forth.

Meanwhile, let us not reverse the normal order of the accomplishment of the great work. Let us not imagine that Woman, as we know her today, is ready to assume the great role that awaits her, but which demands of her that she should essentially become a woman again, that is to say that she should concede to the evidence and recognize that her understanding shines forth from her sex and not from her brain. In our days the woman, wanting to become the equal of the man, has excessively cultivated her reason. That is the great error of the century and the origin of all the evils from which we suffer. In man, Reason replaces Understanding. It is proper to him, and it serves him suitably. But the woman becomes inferior when she follows this example, which is abnormal for her.

The woman must relearn, before governing, to draw forth the spiritual light from her sex, in celebrating the rites that we are advocating. It is thus that she will become again what she has been at each ascensional epoch of history, that is to say each time that the matriarchy has been reestablished (or established). In becoming a priestess, the woman will again become the mother-educator of the man, who will then no longer lose himself in debauchery. She will fecundate him spiritually, instead of weakening him in all his being, as happens today. And in giving moral and physical health back to the man, she will necessarily orient him toward reasonable and just action. Only thus will humanity be able to be cured of its current sufferings.

Succinctly, the program must be the following: 1) building of the first, provisional chapel of the Third Term of the Trinity; 2) reeducation of some women destined to then become the first high priestesses of the new Temple; 3) re-education at the same time of a group of men with a view to re-establishing rites from preceding cycles in their purity; 4) preparation of the public for these new usages by means of literary and philosophical propaganda.

If that is accepted, three to five years will suffice for obtaining the first palpable results.

PART IV

Relations with others

✢

Naglowska knew many esotericists and metaphysical thinkers in Paris, in Rome, in Alexandria, and elsewhere. In addition to her own magical group, she participated at one time or another with several others. While she knew many of the leaders in her field, there were rivalries, and she did not always get along with them. In this part of the anthology, we find her criticizing some that she did not agree with and responding with great wit and humor to those who had criticized her. Here she turns her attention to Krishnamurti, P. B. Randolph, Guénon, and others.

37

LA FLÈCHE

AGAINST
KRISHNAMURTI

This article appeared in La Flèche *No. 5, February 15, 1931. It has an interesting background, because Krishnamurti was the protégé of the Theosophists, and Naglowska herself had for a time been involved with the Theosophical Society, from which she was by this time estranged. Her opposition to Krishnamurti, though, appears to be based on her own teaching.*

Krishnamurti is traveling through the world, imparting a teaching.

The substance of his teaching is non-teaching, that is to say the negation of all systematic ideology that tries to translate Truth to make it accessible to others.

Besides, Krishnamurti says that *"the truth is individual,"* that *"no path leads to it,"* that no one can help another in the search for the profound reason for what is. Every man, every woman, according to the prophet of the theosphists who has denied the theosophists, is absolutely left to him or herself in the terrible torment of the thirst for Knowing, and at this point an impenetrable wall separates individuals, one from another.

He, the prophet who does not wish to be other than "a man, quite simply," can only repeat this one thing: "I have found, but to you who are seeking I cannot say anything at all."

And, indeed, he does not say anything, this Krishnamurti disengaged from theosophical discipline. He travels through the towns, surrounded by his friends, gives lectures to which come hearers without number, and with a charming smile accentuating his long Hindu look, he endlessly repeats: "live, look, feel, flee all limitations, reject all philosophies, do not accept any system, don't let yourself be led by anyone." Essentially: be like infants amusing themselves.

Krishnamurti, we ask you this question: Do you believe that it is possible to organize human happiness—since you are constantly advising people to be happy—with the principle of dislocation of collectivities that necessarily follows from your adoctrinal doctrine? Doesn't it seem to you that the first effect of your preachings must be, in those who love you and for that reason accept what you say, hatred and scorn for all constructive ideas and actions? Don't you believe that, when the majority of your admirers is no longer composed of those who are materially or intellectually rich, who in shedding their skins still keep a certain balance, that is a possibility of living and moving, but rather of individuals who do not yet have anything and for whom, consequently, the doctrine of non-limitation necessarily translates into the conviction that they each have the right to do whatever they please—don't you believe that at that moment, with ferocious and bestial appetites unleashed, we shall see develop the most frightening of antisocial revolutions? Don't you believe, in other words, that your teaching, so sweet and poetic, could become, if the masses attach to it, as its starting point, a furious destruction . . . a little like what we have seen since 1917 in Russia?

We do not wish to tell you that there is not some truth in your idea concerning the inexpressibility of Truth, we do not agree with you when you proclaim that it is not necessary to make any effort toward at least approximate translation of what one has felt and understood as truth.

Humanity as a whole always suffers when it lacks an organization based on a faith, and a faith cannot be born and propagated if an architecturally presented doctrine does not precede it in the beginning. For well-being, always understood by the lower classes as material well-being, is never anything but relative, and men need an ideal that completes what they do not have and draws them elsewhere. Illusion is necessary to be happy even in poverty, and we believe, Krishnamurti, that you do not understand that.

We believe, Krishnamurti, that it is impossible for you to put yourself into the skin of him who suffers because he has been disinherited, and that it is likewise impossible for you to understand the need that so many seekers experience to find a hand that can show them the way.

Yes, you are right when you say that it is impossible to communicate to others the Truth seen by one in its totality, but we assure you that it is preferable to translate what one has seen just the same, rather than jealously keep the consoling truth to oneself.

It is necessary to build, Krishnamurti, it is not sufficient to sing and dance, in this epoch where everything is collapsing and falling to pieces, because a certain phase of the divine life is expired and because another—the third of our Triangle—is coming into play through suffering.

According to us, who believe that it is necessary to rebuild the edifice before everything is dead, your word, Krishnamurti, is an evil: a pretty song that encourages the [Reaper's] scythe.

38

MAGIA SEXUALIS AND *LA FLÈCHE*

Naglowska subtitled this article "To Our Detractors." It appeared in La Flèche *No. 7, November 15, 1931, which coincided with the publication of* Magia Sexualis. *In it she gives an account of the circumstances surrounding her acquisition of the Randolph material and her decision to publish the book.*

❦

In the month of May 1928, I was in Egypt.* A quite remarkable French occultist who had a good following in certain Parisian milieux, came to Alexandria to give a series of lectures. We met, and the occultist predicted this for me:

I would not stay long in Egypt. I would leave the country to return to Rome, but an apparent mishap would push me toward Paris. In the City of Lights I at first went through a quite long period of inconceivable tests, but a last mishap, totally exterior, would cause a

---

*[Naglowska was in Alexandria, Egypt, for about two years, beginning in 1927. —*Trans.*]

precious document to fall into my hands, and it would be the source of my new fortune, spiritual and temporal.

The prediction of the French occultist was from that time on borne out: I left Egypt at the beginning of July 1929; I headed to Rome, where I could not stay more than two months, for lack of any way to support myself; and I arrived in Paris on the third of September 1929, where for four months I would know true struggle *on the pavement.**

But a thing written is realized. In October 1930 *La Flèche* was born, and it brought me some extraordinary meetings. On a street corner, in a busy intersection, an unknown hand held out to me a page of "Madagascar," richly decorated: the prospectus for *Magia Sexualis,* by Randolph, which some publishers who were then traveling proposed at that time to publish, in an unusually luxurious edition that would bring the price to close to 3,000 francs per copy.†

The hand that had given me the sheet of "Madagascar" quickly disappeared, but a voice said to me: "This will be for you, for you are worthy of it."

One knows about the noisy publicity that was made last year at around the same time concerning the secret notes of Randolph, which in November 1930 had not even been translated into readable language, and which had been prevented by various obstacles from appearing, each time it was tried, for nearly sixty years.

I received the manuscript in April, when *La Flèche* seemed to be dying. I translated it, and Mr. Robert Télin, to whom I direct from here the expression of my deep recognition, agreed to publish it, without any of the usual difficulties.

I did not know Robert Télin. On the day that I had picked to make the choice of a publisher, I devoted myself to a magical opera-

---

*[In French, this expression also means to be "on the streets," or "homeless." —*Trans.*]

†[This seems quite excessive. When the book came out, the price was 200 fr. —*Trans.*]

tion, which allowed me to see his name followed by his address—*Au Lys Rouge,* 12, rue de l'Université—in magnetic letters on a list, where twenty other addresses erased themselves at the same time, under an agitated veil of thunder-storm gray.

The next day, at five o'clock in the afternoon, I was at the *Lys Rouge* and a quarter of an hour afterward the publication of *Magia Sexualis* had in principle been decided.

If all the rest was not a miracle, this certainly was.

Magia Sexualis appears today to prove to the skeptics that the royal science of magic is true.

Magia Sexualis will not be, as the distinguished director of the *International Review of Secret Societies* (8, rue Portalis), believed, the bible of the religion of the Third Term of the Trinity, but rather the work to which we will refer all our friends and readers who ardently desire serious documentation on occultism and want—at last!—definitive and scientific proof of the impalpable.

The bible of the religion of our third era will appear too, but in its time. It will be composed of the three volumes that we have promised to our readers since the fourth number of *La Flèche,* but we are not fixing any date, in order to not awaken useless impatiences. Everything has its propitious day.

For the moment, we suggest to each person the rapid acquisition of *Magia Sexualis,* for the edition will be exhausted sooner than one thinks, thanks to the benevolence of some or, perhaps, to the malevolence of others.*

We will not have the leisure to repeat the luminous and practical teachings of Randolph in the pages of *La Flèche,* for another task is calling us.

We shall continue the work of *La Flèche,* whose regular publication is now financially assured, with the assumption that all our

---

*[Thanks also, it seems, to its being originally published in an edition of only 1,007 copies. —*Trans.*]

readers have read and studied *Magia Sexualis* and no longer doubt that from sex, rightly understood and served, truth shines forth.

We reject without further loss of time all calumnious insinuations of which we have been the target during the long forced silence of *La Flèche,* and we throw in the face of those who laugh with pale rage this single response: you dirty what is pure out of fear that your own impurity will be apparent, but marsh mire does not obscure rock crystal. It is your scandalous abuses that prevent you from seeing clearly.

Having said that, we will not further address our detractors, unless they take the trouble to bring the discussion into the area of loyalty.

39

La Flèche

P. B. RANDOLPH

Like the previous article, this appeared in La Flèche *No. 7, November 15, 1931. It contains a surprising amount of information about Paschal Beverly Randolph, considering how little is known for certain. Naglowska signed the article with her own name.*

Paschal Beverly Randolph* was born in New York City on October 8, 1825. The tradition says that he was, on his mother's side, descended from a queen of Madagascar. But this thesis is contested in America, from whence come to us reports that are contrary to those that we've received from the rare groups, scattered through central Europe and Finland, where the magicians of the Temple of Eulis, which Randolph founded in San Francisco on the fifth of November, 1861, took refuge.

Is the question of the source of his Negro blood important for the understanding of the very particular initiation of the man to whom we today render the homage that he deserves?

*[Naglowska always spelled this name as "Pascal Bewerly Randolph." This alternate spelling is sometimes met with today, but I have not been able to trace any use of it before Naglowska's translation. —*Trans.*]

We do not heitate to answer, "yes," for, whatever diehard individual-
ists may say about it, the blood that passes from generation to generation
is a determining factor in the formation of people's will and intellect.

Now Randolph's work, which places the center of human capacities (physical and mental) in the sex, and which did not hesitate to
show, already in the nineteenth century, that on the mental plane the
woman represents the positive pole and the man the negative pole . . .
clearly indicates an origin that is foreign to the white race, essentially
Christic, that is to say negator of the spiritual worth of the woman
and of the sacredness of the flesh.

And it is not strange, for us who are announcing the reprise of
the ascendant march toward the Origin, to discover the precursor of
our mystico-realist revelation precisely in a man in whom the infalli-
ble direct knowledge of the ancient African races and the cold, skep-
tical logic of the Anglo-Saxons so happily harmonized.

For us, Randolph's work itself, still more than the features of his
face, however characteristic, proves that the thesis supported by his disciples in Europe is correct: the author of *Magia Sexualis* was a mulatto.

This, obviously, does not weaken in any way the right of the
United States of America to be proud of the birth on their soil of
this prodigious man.

P. B. Randolph traveled a great deal. At the age of fifteen he was
already feeling the pull of the sea and went to work as a ship's boy
on a merchant ship. He sailed thus for five years, when all of a sudden he was taken with a desire to become a doctor. He returned to
his country, worked without letting up, and obtained, at twenty-five
years, the desired diplomas. He was a good practitioner right up to
the time of his death.

But Europe, Paris above all, attracted him incessantly. General
Ethen Allen Hitchcock, who lived in Paris and to whom Randolph
had been introduced by his friends, the doctors Fontaine and Ber-
gevin, introduced him into the occultist circles of the time, and it
is thus that the future American mage struck up friendships with

Eliphas Levi, Bulwer-Lytton, and Charles Mackey. Later, he was introduced to Kenneth, to R. H. Mackenzie, to Count Brazynsky, to Napoleon III, to Alexis and Adolph Didier, to Count Tsovinski, to General Pelliser, to the Duke of Malakoff, and others.

Randolph was excited about the occult mysteries taught by these men: still, he did not subordinate himself to their school: his blood permitted him more and better. He returned to America, and there created the lodge of the Temple of Eulis, which had several branches in different cities of the United States.

He attracted the fellow-feeling and veneration of President Lincoln, who sent him to Russia, around 1866, apparently to get Alexander II's support for the young republic.

Concerning Randolph's trip to Saint Petersburg, nothing definite has been told by his American friends, but having had the very special opportunity to grow up in an environment, otherwise very sheltered, where the truths discovered by Randolph were known and put into practice, we permit ourselves to say—since all the persons whom this could harm have been dead since the war—that the luminous mage did not fail to create a branch of his San Francisco lodge on the nostalgic bank of the white Neva.

Peace to your soul, oh Princesse Hélène, who gave me the first keys to real initiation! May the new generations profit from it today!

The lodges and circles created by Randolph in America opened and closed several times. One does not know the exact reasons, but from some intimate documents left by the great man, it clearly appears that he carefully chose his adepts and sent packing any undesirable elements that worked their way into his secret groups. Certainly, Randolph did not strive for large numbers, and preferred one person of real value to a hundred mediocrities. The same was true in Europe.

People have talked a lot about the animosity between H. P. Blavatsky and Randolph. Current followers of Randolph, grouped in New York, argue against this occult battle, on the subject of which, nevertheless, some very well-documented details come to us from elsewhere.

Logically, H. P. Blavatsky could not find herself in agreement with the practitioner of sexual magic, for her thought and her work belong in spite of everything to the Christic phase, that is to say to the occult dream that wishes for victory of the spirit over the flesh.

In certain passages of *The Secret Doctrine,* one definitely feels that the creator of modern (Christico-Hinduizing) Theosophy had had some inspirations that almost raised the veil of Isis, but each time it fell before the eyes of H. P. Blavatsky when she tried to translate in current words what she had perceived beyond the lower planes. And the Theosophists of today (see *The Veil of Isis,* by Chacornac) bear witness to the same prudish myopia, against which they could not do anything anyway, for the new grace has not touched them.

Readers who will take the trouble to compare *Magia Sexualis* with the innumerable volumes of the Theosophical libraries will be able to see the difference for themselves.

P. B. Randolph died in 1874,* at the age of 49 years. His son, who lived longer, died in 1928.†

Randolph's widow, very old, is still living, in New York.‡

---

*[This is inaccurate. Randolph committed suicide on July 29, 1875. —*Trans.*]

†[Again, this is inaccurate. Osiris Randolph, who had become a successful surgeon, died on July 20, 1929. —*Trans.*]

‡[Kate Corson Randolph died in 1938, in Toledo. —*Trans.*]

40

"THE DAWN" . . . WHAT A CHILD!

Naglowska had many critics, many of whom seem to have been jealous of her notoriety, and occasionally, as here, she took the trouble to publicly respond to one of them. In this case, it was the editor of a rival occult journal. This article is rather entertaining, and it shows a very human side of Naglowska, complete with a wicked sense of humor. It appeared in La Flèche *No. 8, December 15, 1931. Naglowska signed it with her own name, and in the text below she has italicized her comments in response to those of her critic.*

⊹⊟⊟⊹

I have just received three issues of *The Dawn:* August, September, and October, 1931. They had not been sent to me before because *La Flèche* was not appearing.

The August number of *The Dawn* contains the following lines, concerning me: "Madame de Naglowska, a learned Russian—*thanks!*—is a woman of a certain worth—*thanks again!*—and surely initiated—*oh! oh!*—but I would categorize her as dangerously woman—*these last two words are underlined in* The Dawn *by its timorous editor*—for when one starts with this, one doesn't know at all where one is going—*why don't you stay home then, Don Quixote without a sword?*—She spreads her rancors, her disillusionments, over the astral plane, in her way, which is perhaps not a good way (in intention at least, the fact . . . I don't know)."

If you don't know, dear friend and colleague, let it be.

But no, he goes on. A little higher, in the same column on page three of *The Dawn* for the month of August, we find this ridiculous conclusion: "*The Arrow*, 'magical organ'—*he has never understood this subtitle, for his doesn't have anything magical about it*—belonging to Madame de Naglowska, who gives prominence to satanism and prides herself on it . . ."

Dear Sir, you who do not take the trouble to sign your article, written no doubt as a military parade, lacking any theme for real combat, you prove to me by your premature lines that you have not yet read *La Flèche*, whose seven issues that have appeared up to the present are all available to you in the offices of *The Dawn*.

Read, if you please, understand and meditate . . . we will discuss it afterward.

You like it when people respond to you, you become angry when they do not—perhaps it is because you would like *The Dawn* to be cited every time someone dips a pen into an inkwell—but you are forgetting that in the editorial offices of the world one has other things to do than defend oneself against your cardboard weapons.

For the rest, your accusations are monotonous. You always find satanism among those whom you do not like (but do you even know what it is?), venality (would you by any chance be affected by it?—one easily accuses his neighbor of the defects of which one would like to free himself), and dark designs . . .

I remember quite well having already invited *The Dawn* to send its emissaries to 11, rue Bréa,* for the purposes of an investigation . . . in our offices (if one can call them such!). . . . Our doors are still open, and visitors are still received cordially.

Why torment yourself uselessly? Come and see.

---

*[This was Naglowska's address at the time. —Trans.]

41

MY SPIRITUAL CHIEF

The following article appeared in La Flèche *No. 10, February 15, 1932. Naglowska signed it with her own name.*

In the January 1932 issue of the *International Review of Secret Societies*, M. G. Mariani, the distinguished critic of this "free-catholic" journal, devotes several pages to *La Flèche* and *Magia Sexualis*.

After having reminded his readers of the principles of our doctrine, he writes this: "It is less a matter of judging this doctrine of sexual magic itself than of situating it in its milieu. It is undeniable that, along with precepts that are quite disturbing, one finds passages that may seem acceptable, and which might even have been able to be considered morally uplifting if they were not directed to a society whose education is a Christian education. I shall explain with an example: if a legislator came to preach Koranic morality to us, he would find only libertines and sanguinaries to follow it; at the same time it is undeniable that the law of Mohammed was, for pagan Arabia, a remarkable improvement. In the same way one could say that the sexual doctrine of Randolph and of Madame de Naglowska, preached in certain pagan milieus where the most shameless licence prevailed, might have, in some respects at least, been able to be considered as relatively (very relatively) moral; but announced in a Christian world it represents such an obvious regression that it could find only the debauched and the lost to follow it."

To this opinion of Mr. Mariani—an echo conforming to Christian morality, for which the supreme virtue is virginity, since Christianity represents the period of the divorce between the flesh and the spirit—we respond as follows:

The new religion—the new civilizing era—is presented to humanity not because the latter should find in it any kind of moral progress, but because it corresponds to the new act of the divine drama, specifically in this case to the third act, which is that of the reconciliation of Satan and Christ—of the flesh and the spirit—in the Third Term of the divine Trinity: the Mother.

And, precisely, because many cannot abandon the old, expired regime and resist, consciously or unconsciously, the establishment of the new one—a large part of humanity is destined for destruction in this fatal turn of history. For truth does not intend to be *admitted* by humans: it constrains them to recognize it. Truth is not a beggar that knocks at the door of the profane: she is an empress who triumphs over the rebels.

Humanity finds "good" those things to which it is habituated and "bad" those that require a new effort of comprehension and will. That is why its "opinion" has no essential value and cannot, in any case, serve as a criterion for the judgment of the Religion that is coming. . . .

The same critic, M. G. Mariani, goes on to write this: "I have no reason to doubt her (*Madame de Naglowska's*) sincerity, she is certainly a *medium*, in the vulgar sense. I mean that Madame de Naglowska has a talent for 'seeing'—as one says. This is not as original as one might think—and it is quite dangerous—for a *medium* is nothing other than a *means*: whose *means* is Madame de Naglowska, whom does she obey? She probably does not know—and neither do

I—unless I push the research to the real and ultimate chief of the hierarchy."

It is at this point that the passage that we cited above was placed (page 20 of the January issue of the RISS). As if to suggest, without actually saying it, his secret idea of the "Chief" of whom I must be only the *means,* M. G. Mariani finishes his article thus: "Once again, the orientation of the movement of *La Flèche* only confirms what I have already repeated: of all the occultisms the most dangerous are the imported ones. Let us point out, in passing, that *La Flèche* is announcing a series of lectures whose 'treasurer' is named Levy; it seems to me that I have heard this name somewhere before . . ."

We at once reassure M. G. Mariani and his flock: Mister Levy and his lectures have nothing to do with the movement of *La Flèche,* which, in publishing the announcement in question, was simply obeying the most elementary desire to render service . . . to a colleague. Mister Levy would no doubt be alarmed to learn that someone thinks he is flirting with *La Flèche,* for he is a Jewish convert to Catholicism, and besides, his "powers" are quite problematic.

No, Mr. Mariani, you will not discover the Chief whom I obey, for you will never look where he is to be found, and if I should point it out to you, you would be terrified. My Chief presented himself to me at Rome, papal and Catholic Rome, at the precise time when the conclave proclaimed the enthroning of Pius XI. He was dressed in coarse woolen cloth and a rough cord belted his hips. He was barefoot and had no hat on his head. He gave me a piece of cardboard on which a triangle was drawn, and he explained to me that which I am now unveiling in *La Flèche.* That old man was not of a foreign race, and the Holy Catholic Church knows and venerates his name.

But the hour has not yet come for telling you, Mr. Mariani, the name of him who steered the choice of the present Pope. This is a secret that belongs to *your chiefs,* and if they do not name him for you, I, for my part, will certainly not do so.

And what do you understand by an *imported* doctrine? In the light of the concept of "catholic," national borders should be considered as of diabolical provenance, for it is said in the holy scriptures that there are neither circumcised nor uncircumcised, but all are brothers in Christ.

As to me, I know nothing but humanity and the drama of the divine Breath, which finds there its tragic expression. I know the good who accept the new word and the bad who remain deaf. I declare, what is more, the incurable blindness of those who are afraid from the moment someone speaks to them of something that they do not know: they will not take a step to see that which they have not yet seen, for anguish paralyzes them. So much the worse for them!

42

LA FLÈCHE

SAPPHO, MORE THAN SAPPHO!

Naglowska must have been feeling rather confident about what she could and couldn't do by the time she put out the tenth issue of her little newspaper, corresponding to February 15, 1932. In it she gave space to an article (not written by her) about the German theoretician of homosexuality, Camille Spiess, and to a very controversial lesbian writer, Edith Cadivec. Naglowska wrote the following piece about Cadivec, which was followed by an excerpt from the first of Cadivec's books. The connection she made was that both of them were, in their own way, glorifying Eros.

I find it particularly interesting to situate the work—one could just as well say the life—opposite the thought of Camille Spiess, for the time is now or never to hear the sound of these two bells: Eros praised by a man, and Eros extolled by a woman.

Both of them, also, must be understood beyond what they say, that is to say beyond the *excuse* that they advance to present themselves to the public draped in their respective dreams: Camille Spiess draped in the dream of the Androgyne, Edith Cadivec hidden behind what she calls *dominating maternity.*

Let us leave aside these literary veils, the two typical expressions, in the very essence of their reality. It is there that we shall find Eros . . . adored, though still enchained.

I must explain. Eros is the god of love, and love is the passional transport, which, from the enjoyment of the flesh, draws the individual into the joy of the spirit. To be completely free, Eros must begin from the flesh to fully blossom in the sublime regions where *nothing any longer is, because everything has been conquered.* There begins true knowledge and true creation (the new thing), which is expressed in earthly forms, proper to the limitations, when the fecund ecstacy has ended, and the individual comes back to earth like the eagle after his exploration of the heavens: still blinded by the light from above and drunk with too-great happiness.

But Eros is not complete—he is not completely happy—if his joyous rapture is dulled beforehand by an intellectual will that imposes on him the "story" that he must not "invent" until afterwards.

Camille Spiess dulls Eros with his intellectual constructions relative to the Androgyne, and Edith Cadivec by her care to humanly justify that which she cannot *humanly* do: give birth without the help of a man.

And both of them, Spiess and Cadivec, sing the virtues of Eros, while limiting the latter according to the mold of their individual possibilities: the possibilities of the man who repudiates the woman and the possibilities of the woman who repudiates the man. Why? Because they were born that way.

The thought of Camille Spiess is quite well known in France, but we know much less, one might as well say not at all, the extravagant book of Edith Cadivec, whose translation into French is only now being undertaken and which is destined to appear soon.

The page that we offer here is the first offering to the French reader. It is the least *daring* part of the book, but the most typical as an effort of the author at intellectual justification. The rest of this work is a thing unheard of: a detailed, precise, loyal confession by this woman who is gifted with marvelous qualities but deprived of the essential: duly polarized sex. She has, this astonishing Edith, a sort of double physical functioning, almost a double organ, which she also describes with all the anatomical details. For her this results in a complete incompatibility with the pure masculine polarization, and, consequently, the necessity to want *something else.* But, not being able to offer to Eros his natural bower, she only wants him more ardently. And, indeed, the sexual tension of this woman is formidable, her will strong and sincere, she truly *loves,* though in her own way, and believes, obviously, that she is acting in a superior way. There too, she is close to the spirit of Camille Spiess, who wishes to realize Eros in his third phase without passing through the first two (on the masculine line, that is).*

And while admiring the drama and the very original manifestations of one and the other, I conclude with my old refrain: it is necessary that a man and a woman adore each other totally and reciprocally, it is necessary that the one and the other be healthy and holy, for the spark of victorious knowledge to shine forth from their physical intertwining, only after which the New Life begins.

---

*[This is a bit obscure, but is probably a reference to the three persons of Naglowska's Trinity: the Father, the Son, and the Mother. The meaning would then be that Spiess wants to embody Eros in a feminine rather than a masculine mode. —*Trans.*]

43

"THE SPIRITUAL TREASON OF FREEMASONRY" COMMITTED BY J. MARQUÈS-RIVIÈRE

This article, which appeared in La Flèche *No. 11, March 15, 1932, is a response to a book written by J. Marquès-Rivière,[1] in which he attacked Freemasonry and mentioned (and even quoted) Naglowska's little newspaper as being representative of Masonic thought. Naglowska, for her part, thoroughly ridiculed Marquès-Rivière and denied (at the end of the next article) that she was a Mason. Technically, she was telling the truth, since as a woman she could not be a regular Mason, but there is evidence that she, like some of her former sisters in the Theosophical Society, may have been a Co-Mason. Marquès-Rivière himself had been originally Catholic, then a Mason, and finally returned to Catholicism. During the Occupation he became a collaborator with the Nazis,*

who encouraged his continuing attacks on Freemasonry. Naglowska
obviously wrote this article herself, but signed it with a pseudonym,
"La Flèche."

That a naive young man, having no personal experience of what is commonly called the *mystery,* should come to tell us that he has not found, here or there, the spiritual comfort that he was seeking, and that he should pile insults and imprecations on the men who, according to him, should have facilitated his progress toward truth on the dry path of Knowledge—nothing could have seemed to us more normal—for that is how the vulgar person is made: he is never happy with his meager harvest and sincerely imagines that the veritable truth— the one which he cannot gather himself—must be offered to him by another: *by a man richer than he . . .*

Besides, all the tragedy of the ordinary man comes down to this: he wants to vaunt himself beyond his measure and imagines that the "initiates" owe him the capacities that he does not have. Jesus of Nazareth suffered his share of it, when he was assailed by his compatriots who said to him: "Show us your Father, and we will leave you in peace. But you tell us things that we do not understand."

Is Mr. J. Marquès-Rivière, the author of the shameful work entitled "The Spiritual Treason of Freemasonry," is he a naive young man?

We ask this question in order to know whether we should feel pity or horror concerning him.

For if he is naive, if his "more than seven years" of life as a Freemason have not opened his eyes, if *after* as *before* he does not understand that men are what they are—jealous, envious, egotistical, evil-doers, slanderers, debauched, gluttons, and fornicators—in spite of the grades and titles that they give themselves, and in spite of the color of their flag, which is never more than a dream and has nothing to do with reality, if Mr. J. Marquès-Rivière did not know yesterday and does not know today that *the spirit blows where it will* and does not necessarily come to rest upon the chiefs chosen by humans; if J. Marquès-Rivière is a child irreducibly limited to a threshold of twelve years (normal limit of mental development of the European races), he is worthy of pity, and his book should be considered as the error of an unaware scholar, with no reason to blame him except in the hope of correcting him.

But if J. Marquès-Rivière is more than a child, if he has understood what the Triangle and the symbols of which it is the key mean, his work is cowardice and treachery. In this case, his crime is unpardonable.

For it is cowardly to leave a Society from which one has largely profited and which one does not abandon unless it has not given one enough.

It is cowardly and treason by definition to deliver the secrets of an army, of which one has shared the advantages and the dangers, to another army, from which one will profit now . . . moreover with the same result of unassuaged spiritual thirst.

For Mr. J. Marquès-Rivière throws Freemasonry as feed to the imbeciles, so that he can then leave it and seek refuge in the bosom of the Roman Catholic Church.

Now, he is correct in telling us that Freemasonry, where he was "an officer," combats the Roman Church, and he does not pretend to be unaware that the latter combats the former. He passes, then, from one adversary to the other, where he starts out by betraying.

Should we believe that he has been bought by the priests? Should we believe that he takes this unworthy step out of mere cupidity? Perhaps. We ourselves do not go that far, for having read the 254 pages of the book in question, we wish to believe that Marquès-Rivière is sincere when he says this:

I have not wished to make a "confession"; I have avoided, while speaking as "I," contributing anything other than affirmations.

If the last part of this book is less documented, I apologize. In this area, it is sometimes impressions and oral testimonies that are worth more, for the witness, than books and libraries. I have been a witness of many acts and of many stories.

If Freemasonry had declared that it was a mutual-aid society or a politico-philosophical club, I would have left it in peace, for every social activity can defend its goal. Moreover, I would not have been interested in it, being anti-modern to my very great shame.

But Freemasonry speaks of initiations, of spirituality, of mysticism, of religion, of liberation. It falls therefore within the area of Metaphysics, at least nominally. Now, the practical inside study of this Sect has shown me that its principal goal is a strange reversal of the traditional values that form the very basis of all spirituality. I saw it then in an unhealthy aspect, which only increased after that. I acquired the living testimony, not of an occult plan, which would be inexact, but of the existence of an anti-traditional form of thought, anti-spiritual, anti-Christian. The mask was raised and that is why I have spoken the words "spiritual treason." That this state of spirit may be unconscious, unrevealed, imperceptible, I am the first to admit; that there may be much good faith, much good will, and that they may be at times quite touching, I recognize. But that is not enough. One does not manage the world by good will; it requires will itself. It is necessary to know what one wants, and where one is going. Freemasonry plays on indecision and imprecision—it is its only strength, and it is great. On top of all that, one must add the sleeping potions of occultism, the opium of extravagant and sterile symbolisms, and one understands the strange results that are obtained.

If the danger of Freemasonry were only the creation of nullities and the deification of its foolishness, this kind of business is so common these days that one would be content to just shrug his shoulders. If this Sect contented itself with politics, one could let the "parties" defend themselves by their own means. But behind the attitudes, the buffoonery, the speeches, and the banquets, there is something else quite redoubtable that pulls the strings of all these puppets, and it is this foul odor that I have smelled in the Lodges.

I understood then that at times there were necessary attitudes, obligatory decisions, just and useful executions. I understood the acts of defense; this book is one of them."

J. Marquès-Rivière has quit Freemasonry to defend himself from the *foul odor* that he smelled there, it seems. In the bosom of the Roman Church he will, without doubt, be protected from it.

Anyway, he says himself, after having explained to us in what a subtle fashion the *demonic entities have put forth their tentacles to capture the souls that become animated* and bend them to the service of humanity.

> The Catholic mystical tradition has not fallen into this subtle snare; it has felt that the "creature" had no interest or value except in respect of its relations with the "Creator," and that these relations must be perceived from within and not dictated by a mental or sentimental ideal, no matter how altruistic and charitable it may seem.

Now, fortunate are the rare Catholics who may understand these lines and find themselves in agreement with them. The others—and they are the overwhelming majority—occupy themselves much more with humans and with charity than with God and Love, which makes the Roman Church in its totality human, and worthy of exactly the same critique that Marquès-Rivière directed at Masonry. People are people everywhere, and their defects are always the same. It is in no way necessary to betray one army, exposing it to attack by the other, which is just as human, that is to say: jealous, envious, perfidious, fornicating, and gluttonous. God and His Truth do not gain anything with the victory of the one or the other, and the Joy of Heaven is not realized except when a pure person exalts it with all his body, with all his soul, and with all his spirit at the same time. And the pure one is not better in this church or that, for where he is, his joy shines out, independently of the wickedness of the vile ones who can certainly be found there.

If you don't like the room in which you find yourself, go into the other, but don't condemn those who have received you into the first one. They were not perfect, you say? Foolish one, were you received by the gods?

The human species occupies itself as it can with its public matters; that is its duty, for it is its nature. But you who wish to know the heavens, isolate yourself in your soul and look on High.

Freemason or Catholic, you will understand the same things, if you are worthy of them.

But, to judge by his book, Marquès-Rivière is far from being worthy of *knowing,* for he is afraid of demons and sees them everywhere.

Now, demons are nothing more than the power that the frightened individual gives them. The Fearless Knight annihilates them with a single look.

We hope that J. Marquès-Rivière will acquire, in the bosom of the Roman Catholic Church, the virtues of a Fearless Knight that he has not been able to acquire in the Masonic Lodges. Then, perhaps, he will understand the symbol of the arrow, which he categorizes as Luciferian, on page 175 of his book.*

He will perhaps also understand—when he is no longer haunted by the *Evil*—that the "very closed" group that presides over the destiny of our *Organ of Magical Action* has no need to look for its origin

---

*[In all fairness to Marquès-Rivière, it was the newspaper (*La Flèche*), not the symbol itself (la flèche) that he categorized on page 175 as "Luciferian." I here translate his words, for those who may be interested: ". . . I dedicate the following lines, which I have extracted from a review of small circulation that pertains to a very closed Luciferian group, of Caucasian origin . . ." It is worth noting that the material he excerpted is from an article titled "Isis and Lucifer," which appeared in *La Flèche* No. 3, December 15, 1930, and was written by Frater Lotus (Henri Meslin, who was certainly a Mason and was later also a gnostic bishop). —*Trans.*]

in the Caucasus, for Paris is sufficient for the blooming of all truth.

Concerning the small perfidy of J. Marquès-Rivière, with regard to us, we could have said a lot more, but we prefer to leave this lost soul face to face with his conscience, because we still believe that he has one.

On the other hand, this decorative flower that he has added to the legend that one imagines will drown our young movement, far from harming us, will do us good. The legend, although complete fantasy, adds charm to a sprouting plant, and an evil-intentioned lie is sometimes transformed into truth at the expense of the liar.

We never raise our hand against those who strike us, and it is thus that the blows that are destined for us often fall back upon their author.

44

FREEMASONRY AND CATHOLICISM

This article is a sort of sequel to the preceding one, and it also appeared in La Flèche *No. 11, March 15, 1932. Naglowska signed it with one of her favorite pseudonyms, "Auguste Apôtre."*

La Flèche has just explained the attitude of our group with respect to the inesthetic act of J. Marquès-Rivière.

For my part, I will say here what I think on the subject of the two *Houses of God* that at this moment divide the civilized world into two hostile camps with regard to each other, in spite of the unique spiritual base that binds them together beyond the always-deceiving human appearances.

The two *Houses of God,* Roman Catholicism, on the one hand, and Freemasonry, on the other, possess the truth of the Second Term of the Trinity, the truth of the Son, which separates the flesh from the spirit because of the *divorce* brought to the earth by Christ (read *La Flèche* Nos. 7, 9, and 10).

But, while the Roman Church, whose mission was and still is to express only the pure Christic idea—oh! as pure as possible—subordinates the word of the First Term to that of the Second, and totally ignores the Third Term, whose coming signifies for it the end of the world. Freemasonry, on the other hand, has for its historic task, besides the realization of the Christian idea, the keeping alive of the First Term, of which the Jews are the chosen people, and the preparation of the coming of the Third Term, which will reveal all truths to humanity.

It is because of its mission, so defined, that the more or less official teaching of Freemasonry is by necessity uncertain and at times even contradictory.

Indeed, belonging historically to the Second Term of the Trinity, this Society sees the separation established by Christ between the spirit and the flesh as a *good* thing, and shares, in the ethical and moral domains, Christian sentiment. It officially venerates chastity and considers the woman's sex as the pit of sin.

But, representing, at the same time, the persistent will of the First Term, it is the guardian of the eternal Law of the affirmation of the concrete world—an affirmation wished by the Creator, that is to say by the very Life of God—and in that is near to Judaism. Like the latter, it is rationalist and intellectual, because, desiring life, in spite of the blame thrust upon sex, it is forced to give itself some artificial excuses that form the intellect. Man is *intelligent,* because having denied the natural light, that is to say the devine, he is forced to illumine himself with lamps that he has invented.

In the third place, Freemasonry prepares the future. It does it unconsciously, pushed into it by a force that it does not know except incompletely. It does not know where it is going, but it has faith in its invisible guides. And it is that which it calls: its tradition.

The future, the new phase, presents itself to the eyes of the Roman Catholics as a disappearance of the world, precisely because it is impossible for them to admit, without contradicting themselves, spiritual perfection joined to the continuation of the human race. Man does not come into the world without a previous coitus, but the Perfect, according to Christ, must not indulge in sex. In the city of the Just, according to the Catholic thesis, there will be no new births. To even make Life continue, the immortality of the Just would be needed. That is the source of all the clever Christian inventions concerning the Beyond and the Future Life, after the second coming of Christ upon the earth.

The *tradition,* which is anyway very obscure, of Freemasonry allows for a solution that is at the same time more logical and more divine. It is there that human Reason has truly shown the Mirror of God.

Indeed, the triumph of Christ (or of the Messiah) appears to the eyes of Freemasons under the natural form of a positive event, that is to say in conformity with the eternal Laws. For them, the reign of Christ triumphant is the triumph of Good over Evil within a human framework and without the disappearance of our planet. It is here, in the harmony of the laws that we call *physical,* that the Miracle will be accomplished, the great transformation of humans, who, illuminated by the true Light, will reorganize their existence according to Justice, Mercy, and Truth.

How? No Freemason will answer this question for you, for none of them know the answer. The Masonic mystery is hermetic in this regard, because no Freemason has anything to reveal on the subject. They only know that in duly respecting *every word* of God, that of the First Term as well as that of the Second, the Third Word will come as it must come, according to its natural logic. In that the Brothers of Freemasonry are really algebrists who patiently follow the development of the equation whose solution will be correct, because the givens are exact.

⊣⊨

Now, if some imagine that *La Flèche, organe d'action magique* is a Masonic organization, destined to defend the cause of the Brotherhood, we beg them to disabuse themselves of the notion as soon as possible. Not only are none of us (who sign as La Flèche, Auguste Apôtre, Hanoum, Xénia Norval, and Maria de Naglowska) Freemasons, but it is also very probable that none of the Brothers working in the Workshops would be in agreement with what we have just expounded.

But we affirm this: better than the Freemasons, we know what they are doing and where they are going—for we have received the revelation that they have not, as yet. We have traveled for almost fifty years, and the Light has shown itself to us.

We have lived in Rome, without physically approaching the place reserved for St. Peter and his vicars, and we have heard that which can only be perceived from afar.

We have wandered among the sands of the desert, and we have paid homage to Great Egypt.

The words that have been put into our mouth enclose the total truth of the present hour, and what we proclaim, we understand.

The great Widow has again seen her Spouse. She found him in a tomb, and he dressed her wounds.

The Spouse awakens at this moment, and the second marriage of the Separated will soon be celebrated, to the great joy of all.

Humanity will not suffer much longer. After the last storm, general Peace will triumph.

The Golden Mass will be the concrete consecration of the beginning of the New Era.

45

TO MR. GUÉNON:
WE TAKE UP YOUR
CHALLENGE!

This article, a response to René Guénon, appeared on the front page of La Flèche *No. 13, June 15, 1932. Naglowska signed it with her own name.*

❧

Mr. Guénon, the illustrious collaborator of *Veil of Isis* (Chacornac, 11, quai Saint-Michel, Paris), categorizes our doctrine as "suspect."

Naturally, being illustrious and not considering us to be such, Mr. Guénon does not explain to his readers in what the danger represented by *La Flèche* consists according to him, and sends us a ricocheting rock in this ambiguous, rhetorical form:

> . . . Concerning *La Flèche,* we have ascertained that the article already reproduced by the Notebooks of the Order (October number) had already been published in the anti-Masonic

work to which we made allusion earlier [namely the book by J. Marquès-Rivière with which "La Flèche" occupied herself in our no. 11—Editor of *La Flèche*], but this time, instead of clearly indicating its provenance, it was described only as "extract of a small-circulation review pertaining to a very closed Luciferian group of Caucasian origin."* It is no doubt necessary to magnify the importance of the adversary and envelop him in mystery to give oneself a reason to exist; but frankly, are the anti-Masons who employ such procedures well qualified to censure the charlatanism of certain pseudo-esotericists?

We retain the last few words of this passage, manifestly aimed at us: *pseudo-esotericists,* and we suppose, until there is proof to the contrary, that the illustrious Mr. Guénon is seeking to distance the readers of *La Flèche,* because, according to him, one cannot find on our pages anything but "pseudo-esotericism."

But would Mr. Guénon be capable of telling us how *true* esotericism is to be recognized, and why, if such an "-ism" exists, it is necessary to crystalize it there forever?

Could he think, the illustrious Guénon, that every new idea is dangerous simply because it is new, or because it does not agree with his own teaching?

You see, Mr. Guénon, it seems to us that the world is big enough to contain the *Veil of Isis* and *La Flèche,* without one of these publications being a threat to the other; as far as polemics go, they are not useful except when one holds them within the correct framework of the combat of ideas. That is also the test by which true strength of spirit is measured.

We have declared since our first issue that for us the key of all religious mysteries, as well as the principle of all cosmic laws presiding

---

*[This is the exact description that Marquès-Rivière gave in his book, on page 175. —*Trans.*]

over the unfolding of human history, is found in the life of the evolution of Sex, which is the Root, the Heart, of the Spirit.

All our doctrine is based upon this truth, which we have openly proclaimed without worrying about the hatreds that it could stir up.

We have done it, and we are still doing it because we are aware that humanity has entered into the dark period (predicted by all the Prophets and the Mages of olden times) during which, in conformity with what was foreseen in the Holy Scriptures, the Woman (a woman) must give birth spiritually, rendering to the Man in the form of a new light, that which the latter hid in her since the first day, namely: the mirror reflecting the face of God, which the man could no longer contemplate directly since he had poured out in Eve the spiritual energy, crystallized at the moment of the first coitus.

The Man having caused his fall by abandonment in the woman of the possibility of direct knowledge, no individual of the male sex—even weakened or inverted—can decipher divine truth today, either by intellectual means or by ascesis, which is only a preparation, a period of transitory purification.

For the law of birth by woman, having been established following the Fall from the Father, it is only by woman that the new man can be reborn into the Light, that is to say, re-acquire the capacity for direct knowledge of the absolute.

Within the precise dogma that we thus formulate, there is no malice, nor any ulterior motive harmful to humanity.

By this dogma we are introducing a new thought into the world that invites every man who is desirous of truly penetrating into the spiritual spheres to accomplish with a priestess of the new religion the sacred rite of magical love that returns to the man his lost powers.

If Mr. Guénon is an honest contradictor he will respond to that without banal witticisms and without equivocal allusions unworthy of his talent.

46

LA FLÈCHE

THE "POLAIRES"

One of the magical groups that Naglowska belonged to, at least for a time, was the "Fraternité des Polaires." There is much more that could be said of this group than can be said here, but suffice it to say that Maria eventually became disaffected with the group, as did René Guénon. Other members of the group included Jean Marquès-Rivière, who later returned to Catholicism and became an anti-Mason; Maurice Magre, a journalist who wrote about Naglowska; Henri Meslin, who was also a member of Naglowska's magical group, and a gnostic bishop (Tau Harmonius) as well; Jean Chaboseau, son of Augustin Chaboseau; and the important Synarchists Jeanne Canudo, Vivian Postel du Mas, and Victor Blanchard.* It is not really surprising that Naglowska knew these people; she spent every afternoon with the occultists of Paris. This short article appeared in La Flèche No. 13, June 15, 1932. *Naglowska signed it "M. de N."*

---

*[Most of this information about Les Polaires, and much more, can be found in the very interesting 1995 republication of *Asia Mysteriosa*, by "Zam Bhotiva" (Cesare Accomani). See particularly the introduction to the book, which is by Arnaud d'Apremont.[1] —*Trans.*]

We are pleased to see that the "Polaires" have become more precise in their ideas and—a curious thing—they are visibly coming closer to our doctrine of the Third Term of the Trinity, which they rejected somewhat scornfully when the first numbers of *La Flèche* came out.

We hope that they will soon understand that "The One Who Is Waiting"* will not come only for the Polaires, but for all people worthy of the name.

The great revelation will be made, indeed, in 1933, as we have announced since the autumn of 1930. It is then that the *Entity who is waiting* will choose his elect among the courageous who have thrown themselves into the river of the separation and who are now struggling as they approach the Other Bank. (Read *La Flèche* No. 10.)

The Polaires will then have "their chief with them," just as other groupings will also have theirs.

All these chiefs, meanwhile, will teach the same thing, namely: *all humans are responsible for the act of each, and when the Best shall have conquered Death, all will have conquered it in Him.* It is this word that has been brought to earth by the Crucified One, and it is this that has been insufficiently understood until now. The false brotherhood derives from that.

Now, and to pass to the details of the article in the *Bulletin of the Polaires* of May 9, 1932, we point out to its author that "the new descent (or revelation) of the Father," to which he makes allusion on page 9, must be understood in the opposite sense to the Fall, that is to say as a re-ascending. And the opposite of the Father being the Mother, the Reign that is announced now is that of the Third Term of the Trinity.

For the three successive Names of the active Divinity are: the

---

*[This is Polaire terminology for a messianic figure whom they expected. —*Trans.*]

Father (Fall into Matter, crystallization), the Son (Negation of the Law of the Fall, combat with Satan), and the Mother (Return toward the Origin and reconciliation within the Son of his two natures: Christic and Satanic).

The Polaires still have some way to go, as everyone does in our epoch, for the year 1932 still belongs to the painful period of the struggle of Christ and of Satan.

Christ, in humans, still supports the thesis of purity in chastity, while Satan advocates the light found again in the flesh.

"The One Who Awaits" will prove to men, lost in the intelligence that is detached from the vital source (the womb of the woman), that Truth cannot be attained except by means of the sacred fire of ritual Love.

He will preside over the solemn celebration of the first Golden Mass, and will thus realize Freedom, Brotherhood, and Equality.

Until that day, no one will know the true meaning of those three words.

PART V

creative works

⁜

It is obvious from reading Maria de Naglowska's works, which contained many literary quotations and allusions, that she loved literature. She, a consummate stylist, was a practitioner herself, producing stories, poems, and novelettes and translating the prose and poetry of others. Here, translated into English for the first time, are some of her stories and poems.

47

LA FLÈCHE

POEMS

The first three poems appeared in La Flèche *No. 2, November 15, 1930, under the heading "Modern Russian Poems," and they were signed "by M. de N." The fourth, which is actually poetic prose, is from* La Flèche *No. 6, March 15, 1931, and Naglowska signed it with one of her pseudonyms, "Hanoum." The prose piece is closely related to the first of the three poems and takes several lines directly from it.*

Snow

The snow falls gently, gently,
you don't hear it at all.
These are kisses that fall
like steps.

Your soul leaves delicately, delicately,
you never see a sign.
These are tears one can divine
in the light.

The snow melts, the soul frays,
no one is aware.
Tell me, is there
a heavenly rest?

Facades

There are days when I would like to see you,
for sometimes the nights are cold
and a sad rain begins to fall
against the stones of the facades.

Then I think of your lover and you
and I would like to love her easily,
to be near you sometimes,
and maybe touch you lightly.

Diamonds

Come, tell me your pain,
but be immobile and serene.
I love complaints in vain:
diamonds, too, are vain.

Graze my heart with somber,
vague, and fluid dreads.
I love those white remains:
diamonds, too, are cold.

Play funereal chords
and sing a dirge tonight.
Bard reddened in the Hèbre:*
diamonds, too, are bright.

---

*[This is undoubtedly a reference to her husband, a Jewish musician and Zionist, who left her with three children so that he could go to Palestine. —*Trans.*]

The Silent Fall

You slide . . . a little every day . . . every day a little more . . . into depression, into darkness.

Snow forms in your soul, delicate, invisible at first, invisible a long time, then, little by little it glazes, more and more, and falls.

It's the fall, the silent fall of all that radiated in you at the dawn of life.

The dawn of life! Do you remember? Those bursts of laughter, those joyful frolics, the leaps, and above all, above all, the loves? Do you remember still?

Snow fell then, too, but not in you.

It was outdoors, in the form of subtle flakes, and you, you took them for stars. In you the snow was a scintillation of stars. Stars of gold, stars of silver, stars of emerald.

Why have you let it enter into you, into your sanctuary, into your soul?

Why have you let this cold crystal your dreams, your images, your wishes?

It was fine down there, under the jumbled night sky, forming a cascade of light butterflies falling upon the rigid houses, on the town squares where cross the long, long roads that are never quieted.

It was fine there, in the transparent atmosphere, cruelly cold, strident in its silence.

In you, in you, then, there was no snow, and you loved, you knew how to love.

Now, your soul leaves, delicately, delicately*—you can hardly see—because you have let in the poisoned kisses of the harsh mother, of this Nature that wants to destroy in order to create, to destroy to amuse itself, to destroy for enjoyment, for that is life.

You were not able to resist, nor to open your eyes in time.

---

*[This line is taken verbatim from the first poem in this chapter, "Snow."
—*Trans.*]

One divined tears in the light,* bitter, salty tears, but you, you hardly saw them.

Why, why couldn't you divine them?

The snow melts now as your soul frays.†

Oh! Did the atrocious misery of this spectacle not make you want to die?

To die to be reborn. For there is nothing left for you but that.

One knows nothing, you say, one knows nothing about whether there is a heavenly rest‡ as promised for the great ones, for the small ones too, perhaps.

. . . You don't know anything about it!

Yes, my friend, that is the source of your misery, this fall in your soul of snow that melts and drowns you.

> *Raise your head, my friend.*
> *Rouse your courage.*
> *Listen again to this:*
> *The snow was a flood of stars, it became ice and*
>   *water; rouse it, send it back . . . roses will*
>   *decorate you then . . . perhaps.*

---

*[This line is another reference to the poem, "Snow." —*Trans.*]

†[Another reference to the poem. —*Trans.*]

‡[Another reference to "Snow." —*Trans.*]

48

HORIESE AND FELIX

This is an unfinished story that appeared in La Flèche *No. 13, June 15, 1932. It was subtitled "Symbolic Story—Sixth Arcanum," which refers to the sixth arcanum of the Tarot, which is The Lovers. "Horiese" is an ancient Egyptian name, befitting a priest or priestess. At the end of the story it says "to be continued," but it never was. Naglowska signed it with one of her pseudonyms, "Hanoum."*

The sea was very rough when Felix finally decided to challenge the waters with his swimming.

He could have done it sooner, during the months of summer, for example, when the sky was propitious and the crystalline surface did not oppose human effort, but such was Felix's destiny: he must not undertake great things except at the most difficult moment. His "happy" name had no doubt earned him this destiny . . .

The sea was very rough. Enormous waves pushed one another with an infernal frenzy, in a hurry to shoot the excess of their foam into the greenish crevasses.

They were arriving on the shore like walls of transparent marble, crashing noisily on the damp and desolate sand.

The sky was heavy, dark gray.

Felix was standing, arms crossed on his chest. He received the glacial ardor of the wind full in his face, but his body was warmed by it.

"Yes," he said to himself, "I need real danger to attempt the experiment."

And he imagined, coming out of the waves, the impalpable silhouette of the unreal woman who, during a ferocious coitus that he was consummating with a savage lover, brusquely stopped him in the middle of his amorous effusions and said to him in an imperial voice: "I don't want your death in the arms of this unworthy creature. I'll receive you in my castle and teach you something else, if you swim there."

Felix then left the bed of shame to respectfully interrogate the divine apparition, but his frightened lover brought forth unworthy words and so ruined the spell he had been under.

The lover left and did not come back; but in the soul of Felix there was a storm.

He wanted to know where the castle of the impalpable fairy was, and the waters that he would have to swim across.

He searched a long time and finally found someone to whom the woman had appeared under the same circumstances. That someone pointed out to him the road that he would have to travel to the shore where he now found himself . . .

He had arrived on a sunny day, and he had been able to spot, far off, the marvelous isle where the fairy's castle was built. But he lacked training and gave up the idea of the long swim, although the season was propitious.

Felix loved storms, but the monotonous calm weakened him . . .

He looked at the furious waters, joyfully received the icy wind, and his courage rose within him.

"One more wave," he said to himself, "and I'll throw myself into the currents."

The wave arrived: enormous, menacing, cold. It spit a grayish spume and roared with anger and rage.

That only lasted for a brief instant, but it seemed to Felix that the wave contained all the malefic forces spread through the world: all the forces that oppose the freedom of the spirit, the royal enfranchisement of Man.

The wave broke at the feet of Felix, and, crazy with joy, the young man threw himself into the sea.

Certainly, consciousness must remain silent if the other voice, that of the spirit, is to triumph.

Ordinary consciousness is limited. It knows its weakness in the face of the imperial caprice of Nature; that is why it trembles and becomes fearful when it is necessary to act in a way other than usual.

Intellectual consciousness has no foothold except on the rigidity of the laws of death. Life surpasses it.

Felix quieted his discursive consciousness, as he fought with an unusual heroism against the rage of the sea. He gave free rein to his elementary forces, those that desire, those that are life, and thus triumphed in the terrible test.

He arrived at the other shore because his combat with the unchained currents was in reality a game of love with them.

He fell upon the flowered grass like a sword of steel.

Naked, immobile, his arms extended to the right and left, he lay under the cheery sun of the other shore like a fetish that wants nothing, but can do everything.

In him Life was free and the intellect vanquished . . .

It was then that Horiese, the new Sophia, approached him.

Through the imprecise vapor of her light vestment, the sun kissed her whole body.

Her golden hair was tied back above her neck in the manner of ancient Greece.

Horiese fixed her gaze with its metallic reflections upon Felix and said to him without any passion: "I salute you, man of courage! You have conquered the waters, you are worthy of my love. . . . Rest yourself upon the grass of my island, and when the sun shall have nourished you sufficiently, come into my castle. . . . You will find the key to my door between the two columns of a fountain that you will look for this evening . . . now rest.

Felix hadn't moved during the brief speech of the strange woman. Afterward everything seemed natural to him, and he knew that nothing was impossible for him. Indifference reigned in him like a calm sheet of water in a blue lake.

The queen of the marvelous island remained near him for a few moments. The expression on her face did not vary, and it was obvious that she did not wish any response on Felix's part.

Slowly, she distanced herself, like a golden cloud, leaving behind her a trail of aromatic breath that grazed Felix's sides with a serpentine tickling.

Soon afterward, Felix was sleeping dreamlessly.

When he woke up, the sun was already setting. Long, violet shadows traced regular designs on the green grass.

In the distance, the sea chanted its evening canticle, rhythmed to the calmed breath of the storm.

The sky was absolutely clear: red in the west, fading blue in the east.

Felix did not think about what had happened.

He got up and made a sweeping movement with his two arms, breathing deeply.

He felt stronger than ever, peaceful, well rested.

His mood was joyous.

"It's funny," he thought, "I haven't eaten since yesterday, I've made a fantastic effort, but I don't feel any hunger."

That was when he remembered the marvelous queen and the brief words she had said at his arrival on this shore.

"Indeed," he said to himself, "here the sun no doubt replaces nourishment. So much the better!"

. . . And, human curiosity returning to him, Felix decided to explore the country where he was.

The vegetation was abundant. The large palm trees predominated, but there were also tufted bushes upon which splendid flowers blossomed, giving off a very special aroma.

Felix determined that there was no other human or animal there. The animal kingdom was not represented on this island except by many birds of magnificent plumage. They came in all sizes, enormous and minuscule, and each bird gaily sang its special melody.

The works of Man were nowhere visible.

"Still, the queen had spoken to me of her castle, and about a key that I must find near a fountain . . . a strange enigma."

Now, Felix's curiosity was really piqued, and at the same time a dull thirst pressed at his throat. The fountain? He felt an imperious need to search for the fountain.

To do this, he covered the whole island patiently and in concentric circles.

He remarked, then, that this land was like the summit of a cone whose base was lost in the water.

Night was now very near, but he had not found the fountain.

Neither was the castle anywhere to be seen.

Felix's thirst grew from minute to minute. He now discerned its nature.

"The queen had only a light, vaporous vestment, and the sun kissed her body," Felix said to himself, seeing clearly in his imagination the harmonious contour of Horiese's flanks. "Does she disappear when night comes?"

This idea lit a terrible flame inside Felix.

"Have I conquered the waters and absorbed the sun to arrive . . . too late?" he asked himself, while the night became darker and darker around him. "Now, no light guides me at all, and I'm devoured by interior fire in the middle of this uninhabited island, plunged into the shadows . . . even shouting wouldn't help . . ."

He was on the point of giving up when a perfumed breeze came to his nostrils.

"Ah! It's her perfume!" he shouted. "What is your name, oh marvelous queen? Reveal your name to me, so that I can evoke you . . . Where are you? You are devouring me like a perfidious fire, you undress yourself in my view . . . Have you made me come here at night just so that this would be impossible?"

The conqueror of the waters grieved like the weakest of men.

49

LA FLÈCHE

THE CRY OF MAN

This short work appeared in La Flèche *No. 15, February 15, 1933.
Naglowska signed it with the pseudonym "Xènia Norval," which she
had also used for the original serialization of* The Sacred Rite of
Magical Love. *The first part of it is a sort of prose-poem, which is
followed by the statement "This poem belongs to no one. No one is the
author of it." But at the end of the work, Naglowska wrote "All rights
reserved for all countries."*

※

*Woman! . . . alone! . . . You, who walk there! . . .
    Why this luminous look? . . . Old and young,
    handsome and ugly, they follow you step by step,
    and I, song of the immense sea of races living,
    dead, triumphal, fallen, and massacred, I come
    too . . . why?
I want, I take. Behold your white face in my browned
    hands. I bend your body, I make it tractable, I
    hold your soul in my fingers . . . and you? . . . Ah!
    You see only me . . . why?*

Peace? You wanted to give me peace? The burning
peace of your haggard fire, scattered over your
brow and on your breasts and in your hair . . .
everywhere!
Oh! Fool, I roll upon your body . . . I hate your soul
. . . beautiful! . . . Be a rebel or die! Consume
yourself in my fury and have no fear of the
black chaos that awaits you there, the only peace
. . . Serpent of anguish! Beautiful lie! . . . Oh!
Nothing effaces the fatal seal: the water that runs
there, the willow that remains, the moon that
is veiled, and the stars that titillate your spirit,
all of that bespeaks your cruel fate. Go, weep, or
elsewhere begin again this infinite pain . . . until
the tomb, until old age . . . but cease to alarm me
thus!

This poem belongs to no one. No one is the author of it.

⁂

A woman pulls away from a man at the moment of supreme ecstasy, on a summer night, at the edge of a narrow lake.

They have known each other for only a few days, but since the first evening the woman has said to the man, "If I fall into your arms anyway, it will be so much the worse for you, for then I shall steal your work from you and your most beautiful poem will be spoken by me—the poem that you have not yet written."

The man was a poet and the woman a priestess of the Temple of Love.

He wanted it anyway, and he threw her to the ground, on that hot summer night, at the edge of the lake. But suddenly and when he was returning with difficulty from the incredible intoxication that he had felt, she stood up in front of him and, like an accomplished artist, spontaneously recited to him the poem that you have just read.

The woman in question had never written any verse, neither free nor classical. He, the poet, recognized that, indeed, the poem unveiled his most secret thoughts.

Neither of them dared to sign this "Cry of Man," which is the fruit of their ecstasy harmonized according to the Laws: the woman plunging her dream into the consciousness of the man, while he lost himself in her corporeally. If he was prepared, he would have gotten his poem himself.

50

THE TEMPTATION
OF PITY

This short story was serialized in La Flèche *Nos. 16, 17, and 19, corresponding to March 15, 1933, April 15, 1933, and March 15, 1934. Naglowska signed it with one of her pseudonyms, "Hanoum."*

Come! On this warm night, I want to give you my blessing; you have been patient for so long, and you ask if we are forgetting you . . . Dear Disciple! In the ardent chapel, no name inscribed is ever neglected, but the more worthy the student, the more noble, the longer is the wait that one makes him endure.

Besides, my friend, in the court outside the Temple where your personal work is accomplished, this hand that I now lay on your head could not be of any usefulness. This hand confers upon you the mysterious force, the flame obtained at the magical Mass, which the fire that burns in your mortal flesh must be able to transform into synthetic light. But if the work of the man is still imperfect, divine grace cannot aid him. . . . Soon enough, in the presence of the witnesses to your test, a Freed Hunter will ask you the way. If your glass is well made and your oil very pure the wick that I light will be able to illumine you. But if by misfortune, and in spite of your studies, you do not know how to distinguish your left from your right, dear disciple, you will leave there covered with shame, and in the court, you will still sweep. On your personal path, no one can hasten your progress, and He who awaits shows you no preference. You shall cross the threshold if you are worthy, you shall not cross it if you make a mistake.

"Meanwhile, and since I am your future lover, the virgin destined to extend herself in front of you, so that together we may form the rectangle, if you make a mistake, my friend, I shall take you in my arms. I shall revive you, oh dear disciple, with a thousand kisses of my purified mouth. I shall speak into your ear the word of the enigma because I don't want your shame. I don't want to go back in front of your image hanging in the Temple on the wall reserved for the non-freedmen. I don't want my sisters, seeing my sadness, telling each other in a low voice, 'He has not succeeded.' For, look, the Freedman, who soon shall ask you the way, will return later on another horse. If the blessing that I now give you is not efficacious and you do not guess, on his return you will be able to answer, and then, oh my dear, great will be my joy . . ."

A virgin consecrated to the Temple of Love said these things to a man being tested, and the branches of the trees swayed softly in the garden called "of temptation." The man was a young apprentice of the Brotherhood of the Knights of the Golden Arrow, and the woman, a priestess of the first degree of Magical Wisdom.

She was still speaking, and in a more and more amorous voice, when the examiners, in dark hoods, came through the alley, under the secular oaks. They marched in single file, and when they had arrived at the testing place, they arranged themselves in a semi-circle around the young couple. Some moments passed in the deepest silence, then, a sharp whistle cut through the air, and a horseman appeared, dressed as a hunter. He stopped his mount in front of the group and cried out in a strong voice: "May your mercy be with me, oh my friends gathered here! I have lost my way, and I no longer know on which side the good route is to be found. Outside, the storm roars, and all is confusion and terrible suffering. Mothers are complaining because they no longer have bread to give to their children, and men prowl the streets of the town like hungry wolves. One speaks of war, of revolution, of fleets burning on the sea, and houses collapse because of malefactors. I saw all that and doubt entered into my heart. I ask myself whether I should revolt against those who profit from the misery of others or against those who, in spite of this misery, still envy the fate of the wealthy, for neither the one nor the other seeks to know the profound reason for all these calamities, and they do not try at all to again become just. I do not know on which hand the good cause is to be found, and because this doubt has entered into my heart, I come here to ask you to which side to orient myself. Answer me, you who know!"

Then the man being tested stepped forward and answered the horseman thus: "Brother freed from the drudgery of the courtyard, man freed of human hindrances, I will try to answer you according to my understanding, frankly, without any subterfuge. I still sweep in the court of obedience, and my wisdom is limited, but here is what I think: all revolt is sterile, save the revolt against those who show us pity, for only that one strengthens nobility of the heart. Freed Hunter, if it is true that you have lost your way in the human fray from which you return, here is my counsel as a young apprentice: revolt against all those and be among them the hunter who hunts all beasts without distinction—the hungry beasts, because they think only of their hunger, and the satiated beasts, because they think only of creating new appetites for themselves. Both are unworthy of Him who waits for us in this Temple of Love, and it is their wickedness that prevents us from hastening our presence before Him. That is why we revolt against them all, we go neither to the right nor to the left, but we climb the slope of the Mountain. Let us put right the ascending line of the Triangle, and let us proclaim the new Truth . . .

"And do you believe that you all alone can accomplish this gigantic work, climbing the slope of the Mountain, setting straight the Third Angle, the ascendant line of human history; are you multiple? Are you in everyone? Because listen, oh younger brother, you who are still sweeping in the court of obedience of the Golden Arrow: no individual perfection is a historical value if it cannot be extended to others in such a way as to lead them beyond themselves, beyond their misery, beyond their ignorance; that is the cruel lesson that life teaches us. . . . Here, in the shadow of the Temple, each sweeper-novice devotes himself to a vain task if he does not at the same time acquire the capacity to transform people by virtue of his own example. In this court you shake the white powder off yourself, the remains of the crumbled edifice of the Second Era; you acquire the noble dark virtues, the courage, the interior rigidity that is hidden behind the mask of politeness, the correct view of things veiled and deep, and you learn to love the future more than the past; but these superb, dark qualities can do nothing, if they do not shine like clean and transparent gold; if they remain opaque in you. . . . Oh disciple, the Lord who awaits us in this Temple, behind these walls from which he cannot leave unless carried by a great human current, has need of a King and not of a miserable one who knows only how to discourse; for a King wields subjects and armies, while the erudite only show off words. Now, everything is only words and vain discourse, if a movement of real liberation does not take shape among the crowds who follow a true Chief, and that is what the question was about that I asked you earlier: where is the route to become King? . . . It is neither to the left nor to the right, so you said; for to the left reigns the hypocrisy of the cheapened values of the Second Term, charity, pity, goodness, proclaimed to better enrich themselves and to make others sink still lower, and to the right it is artificial and therefore unhealthy reconsolidation of the aged walls of a Church without spirit . . . To climb the slope of the Mountain while bringing the crowds after you, to build the Third Temple whose twelve gates will be open to all so that God may be there, how to do this? For Satan, the Great Prisoner whom we glorify in this enclosure when we touch our foreheads, grants us the knowledge useful to our individual improvement; but for his pain to cease and with it our contraction of the brain, something else is still needed . . . but where to find it? No one will climb the dangerous slope of the Mountain if he has not first conquered this key."

The Freed Hunter of the Brotherhood of the Golden Arrow offered this last word in a particularly strong voice, exhaling the word "conquered" like the breath of a storm wind. It seemed then to the Apprentice that the rows of secular buildings along the dark alley repeated this word and that the moon gliding among the thin clouds hastily veiled itself, stricken by modesty. Something very cold disengaged itself from the semicircle of the examiners, none of whose features could be seen under the hoods; the future Lover herself seemed indifferent to what was happening. The Apprentice tested on this warm night was not a contemptible fellow, and the solemn moment did not shake his dignity. He took a step forward and, extending his arms to the right and the left like a man who had decided to brave all dangers, he answered firmly: "Since the key of the Great Mystery cannot be found except by one alone, given that a King suffices, older brother, may it not displease you, if I knew the secret I would not tell you . . ." A shudder went through the dark hoods of the examiners, and one of them said to his neighbor: "He is solid." He to whom this reflection was addressed raised his shoulders without saying anything, but another observed with the tone of a chemist examining a stone: "Would he speak the same way if he saw with his own eyes what the Freedman is telling him?"

In single file, the examiners left as they had come, mute under their black hoods, impassible, like inanimate stones. One saw them snake, like a long string of dark pearls, along the edge of the ravine, which encircled the temple of the Great Prisoner with a sinuous abyss. The moon illuminated them with its bluish glow. It also illuminated the Freed Hunter, who, troubled by the prideful response of the apprentice who had been tested, was now distancing himself at a furious gallop of his white courser from the garden of temptation. The noise of the horseshoes striking the dry ground of the main road arrived at the ears of the young Sweeper of the Court of testing of the Brotherhood of the Golden Arrow like a bitter reproach. . . . And still his reason told him that he had behaved himself in every detail of the first test in conformity with the teaching that he had received in these three years of waiting during which he had conscientiously swept all that, in his thought and in his heart, did not find a justification in conformity with the severe satanic doctrine that wishes that each candidate for admission to the second degree should never act without knowing why and should always be aware of what is useful or not to the liberation of the Great Prisoner chained within the cave of the human temple. . . . "I have done what I had to, and I took reasonable positions," he said to himself in an atonal voice, still it does seem that brothers superior were expecting another answer from me . . ."

"Indeed," answered the future Lover, "the white courser of the Freed Hunter is galloping on the road without knowing where his horseman is leading him . . ."

"What do you mean? Your words are enigmatic and still less clear than the shadows of this garden. Does the horseman know at least where his mount is going?"

"He will return here, as I told you, but if you still don't know how to answer, oh my friend, it will be heartrending. . . . You heard what he said: one speaks of war, of revolution, the children have nothing to eat, the women are in a panic, the men prowl like menacing wolves. The Dawn is approaching, little time is left to us. The last great war is announced. The two armies line up. Which side will you be on? See, I tremble when I say that, because for three years my fate has been tied to yours, and if you go to the left, I will be pulled to the left, and if you go to the right, I will be pulled to the right, but I will not be able to be true if you are false. . . ." She was as white as an unreal specter and her pain was sincere. Her large eyes with their widened pupils had an astonishing fixity and seemed to look inside and not outside. The green gown that enveloped her from the throat to the ankles made her look like a stem that keeps nothing for itself and sends all toward the flower: her head. Thick blond hair framed the pale face, held by the wide, golden string fillets adorned with arabesques and decorated with fine precious stones, chosen wisely according to the laws of the high magical sciences, to which the priestesses of this temple of Satan consecrate themselves. She was beautiful like cold things that excite the brain, but do not direct themselves to the heart. Because of that her moving speech troubled the young man being tested, but did not shake him. He crossed his arms over his wide chest and began to reflect. The future Lover, respecting his meditation, backed away a few steps and, throwing her head back, offered her open eyes to the rays of the moon.

51

LA FLÈCHE

THE LOVE
OF THE PRIESTESS

*This is Naglowska's last major piece in her little newspaper. It
appeared in the last issue,* La Flèche *No. 20, January 15, 1935.
In its form, it is very reminiscent of Evola's "Poem in Four Voices,"
which Naglowska had translated from Italian into French for him
in 1920 (it has survived only in her French translation). There is
something very touching about this poem (not easily translated,
because it is heavily dependent upon rhyme), especially when we
take into account the circumstances of her life. She was ill and
weakening, and in a little more than a year, she would be dead. In
a way, it is her farewell to us.*

⚜

*A storm-blue island. A leaden sky. Slowly, the Priestess advances on the
dry and hard path. Her mantle drags, lengthened, on the dusty pebbles,
her harp sings strangely, grazed by the branches. Her voice, vague, mur-
murs this:*

THE PRIESTESS. To me, so frail,
Why this heavy load?
The freezing night?
The glorious pretense?
My feet, so small,
Fear the hard hillocks.
I fear the sounds that grate
on this sinister wall.
Oh! Do not call me, ferocious Spirit!

And, from the shore, the crowd comes running happily:

CROWD. She is collapsing!"
"She is weeping, I believe!" "Who then says that it is a god who
believes?"

Poetry, a vaporous shadow, extends her protecting arm. Drama, sumptuous, and Comedy, frivolous, place themselves to the right and left of the Priestess. Are they men or women? Useless question. Here is Genius, looking serious, detaching himself with authority from the mass of the excited clouds. Long, indecipherable sighs pass through the air.

POETRY. She has sung my songs.

COMEDY. She laughed my laughs.

DRAMA. On the trembling stage,
She knew how to speak my heart.

THE CROWD. And says nothing at home.

GENIUS. The crowd is vile.
Flee its evil eye.
When, servile,
It spews out its licking
And deceitful compliment,
May one purge the isle!

The humans fall to the rear, like a mooing herd. They say:

HUMANS. I think, brothers, that the genius, in the evening, with no mystery about it, like anyone, is going to see a gossip. (*Coarse laughs.*) And I say, certainly, that the priestess, acquiesces to nocturnal drunkenness—Quite simply!—And is restless afterward! Oh! Oh! If one only knew!—What then?—I'll keep the secret.—But what is it that he knows?—Rumor had it one day. . . . But that was not at all for sure, and was even denied!—Flowers lose their smell, when the fruit is ripe." (*They go out.*)

GENIUS. The faint-hearted have left these sacred spaces.

VOICES IN THE CLOUDS. The echo follows them still!

GENIUS. Sonorous voices awaken in the night and create. Priestess, arise!

THE PRIESTESS: Priestess, I was that. My songs are dead!

DRAMA. To this agreement I bring a broken heart.

POETRY. We shall make a hymn of it, do you want to? A proud hymn of passion vanquished.

THE PRIESTESS. I shall vanquish no more.

COMEDY. I surprised upon the sea.
A ravishing couple.
Any faithful landmark
Made the sport pleasant . . .

THE PRIESTESS. . . . in comedy!

GENIUS. Pity the holy woman.
Pity the bold flower.
Here to sound the scale

Of her hardened sorrows.
Talents, do you withdraw?

The Talents withdraw. Here are their reflections from the back of the scene:

POETRY. I told her
    That I love the greenness
    When pure waves
    Smile from the seas,
    The beautiful sun,
    That does not see our tears,
    Always seeming the same,
    Bathing our cries of alarm
    In warm rays.

DRAMA. But her?

POETRY. I saw nothing of her
    But the drawing,
    Adorned with pearls,
    And with a fiery wake.*

They exit. Genius and the Priestess are alone. The night is very dark. At times the wind blows. The clouds regroup, taking laboriously human forms.

GENIUS. Look at you, without talents.
    Woman! Only woman!
    Sluggish and slow,

---

*[An alternate French translation/double entendre: And with an ardent furrow. "Furrow" is usually used of a plowed furrow, or a ship's wake, or a track. This could represent the Priestess's hoped-for legacy. The Priestess, of course, is the now-flagging Naglowska herself. But this may also be intended as a play on words, for "furrow" could also represent a woman's labial cleft. This, in turn, could be a reference to the public's association of Naglowska with sex. —*Trans.*]

Your dreams take flight in the wind
Like smoke without flame.

VOICES IN THE SKY. Those were souls.

THE PRIESTESS. I am only a leaf that trembles,
A tear that hangs from a lash,
An ephemeral image that seems
Quite superb, but is only made of clay.
Still, I please myself that way!
THE VOICES. There are in the skies
Voices in mourning,
That sorrowing
Do receive
This mystery
Of the heart that passes
And which grows weary
Of its happiness.

GENIUS. Tell me now of your sorrow.

THE PRIESTESS. No! It is not a sorrow!

THE VOICES. The hour is sounding!

After a moment the Talents come back. One can barely see them, but one guesses their inquietude:

THE TALENTS. What will she say?

THE VOICES. Who then is afraid of the summoning chant?

POETRY. I take up my lyre.

COMEDY. And I take flight.

DRAMA. I shall stay, but I'll be silent.
Lower the curtains of cloth.

The soul of Life now appears.
Kneeling, let us hear its strophes.

GENIUS. Speak!

Silence. The Priestess collects herself. A dream is kindled in her eyes. Her arms rise slowly, and her knees bend.

THE PRIESTESS, *on her knees.* When I am near Him,
   He is so large and my eyes so small,
   That I bend my head low,
   He believes then that I do not love Him.
   When I am alone in a field,
   My soul rears up like a volcano,
   My mad cries of love are carried off,
   And only the echo speaks softly to me.
   But, yesterday, He was in the court.
   I had my harp and my most beautiful attire.
   I broke strings and tore fine veils,
   And madly I kissed his two hands.

HUMAN VOICES. Oh! Crime!

CELESTIAL VOICES. Oh! Dream!

GENIUS. The gods, respectful, arise.

THE PRIESTESS. And He, Superb, smiled!

THE CELESTIAL VOICES. Do you hear this immense cry?

OH! Poetry! What were you doing?

THE ECHO. For virtue . . . ?

THE HUMANS. No, for shame.

GENIUS. Silence! Glory!

THE PRIESTESS. And his bright smile pleases me.

A HUMAN VOICE. What did he say?

THE PRIESTESS. Oh! I don't know!
    They came and I wept,
    With joy, perhaps . . .

THE HUMANS. Or with bitterness.

The crowd detaches itself cleanly against the gray-mauve backdrop. The mocking sneers are abject.

THE PRIESTESS. My soul smokes in a holocaust.

THE HUMANS. Will we see again Faust and Marguerite? And then, what follows!

The priestess remains silent. The indignation of the Talents is vibrant.

GENIUS. The crowd wants the rite
    Of its mediocrity.
    In its simplicity
    Love is unusual
    To its mentality.

Poetry advances, followed by Drama and Comedy. Placing one knee on the ground and presenting her lyre with a moving gesture, she says:

POETRY. Here are your words, projected
    Upon my lyre.
    A whole empire
    Is in thee reflected.

PART VI

contributions of Julius Evola to *La flèche*

A fair number of writers besides Naglowska wrote for La Flèche, *often using pseudonyms that now make it difficult or impossible to identify them. Foremost among these other writers was Julius Evola, whose close relationship with Naglowska is well known. One guesses that Evola wrote these two pieces as a favor to Naglowska, but it seems significant that he did not hesitate to sign them with his own name. The second article appeared in what is one of the rarest issues of the little newspaper. It has probably not been seen since the 1930s. Here, then, are the two articles that Evola wrote for* La Flèche.

52

OCCIDENTALISM

Julius Evola wrote this article for the very first issue of La Flèche, *October 15, 1930. It is characteristic of his thought, and quite forcibly expressed. He would later write another piece, for the third issue of the little newspaper. He signed this one "J. Evola."*

He who has, clear in front of him, the sense of *occidentality* and strives to maintain it, as a living growth with neither mixture nor alteration, sees advancing today, along with materialism, a new and more subtle danger: *the spiritualist threat.*

Indeed, never as much as today has the West had so much difficulty finding a precise orientation, in accordance with its traditions, and that above all because of the singular conditions that the West itself has created.

On the one hand, we now see in the West a world of affirmation, of individuality, of realization, as clear vision (science) and as precise action (technique), but this world knows no light, its law is that of fever and agitation, its limit is matter, the voice of matter, abstract thought applied to matter. On the other hand, a push toward something higher is accentuated, toward a "not that," but this impulse ignores the law of affirmation, the value of individuality and of reality, and is lost in indefinite forms, mystiques, of abstract universalism, of rambling religiosity.

Where the West affirms the active principle, warrior, realist of its tradition, it is therefore deprived of *spirit;* and where it aspires to spirituality, it no longer has present in front of it this fundamental principle of occidentality and gives place to its opposite; the mist of neo-spiritism invades it with its esthetico-orientalizing, theosophico-spiritualizing, christianizing, moralizing, buddhizing evasions, which contradict all, like a very new, exotic rudeness, the virile spirit of occidentality.

This state of affairs has become a sort of artificial dilemma, which is one of the deep roots of the crisis of the modern West. Understanding that is the first step. Finding an alternative is the condition for health.

The spiritualistic reaction to the reality of the modern world certainly has a right, but it no longer has it when it includes in the same negation things that are different, losing the sense and the spirit that, through the experience of realism, have been realized by the Occident as an almost general state of consciousness. The realistic modern world, as spirit, is intensely occidental. Its realization empties, indeed, into the arimanic kingdom of the machine, of gold, of number, of metropolises of steel and cement where all contact with metaphysics dies, where is extinguished all sense of the invisible and living forces of things; but through all that, the occidental soul has confirmed and strengthened itself in a "style" that is a value and before which the plan and the forms of purely material realization—which, alone, are immediately visible—can be considered as a contingent envelop of which one may make abstraction and which one can attack and beat down without suffering in any way.

It is the attitude of science, as experimental knowledge, positive, methodical, in the place of all instinctive intuitionalism, of all confused and superstitious clairvoyance, of all interest in the indeterminate, the ineffable, and the "mystical." It is the attitude of technology, as exact knowledge of the controlling laws in the service of action, by virtue of which, certain causes being put into place, there follow certain determined and predictable effects without intrusion of moral, sentimental, or religious elements, in place of prayer, of fear, and of aspiration to "grace" and to "salvation," as also of all Asiatic fatalism and of Semitic messianism. It is the attitude of individualism as a real sense of autonomy, of healthy warrior pride, of free initiative, in place of the communistic and fraternizing promiscuity of traditional dependence, in place of personality-less universalism where contemplation prevails over action, and the pluralistic world of forms is suffered as the death of the "One."

Although they are very diverse in their forms and degrees, in all the characteristic realizations of the modern world there operates an impulse in conformity to these three fundamental dimensions of the occidental spirit. *The error has been to confuse them with the materialism of the realizations to which they have been applied.* Every reaction to materialism, every will to surpass materialism has since become associated with a misunderstanding of the spirit of occidentality; the reawakening of "spirituality" has been translated by a search in one or other exotic belief, with a gradual evasion of the occidental laws of realism, of action and individuality, giving place precisely to this contemporary neo-spiritualism, which, if it even retains anything truly spiritual, remains for us—we declare it without hesitation—a sort of peril, as well as an element of degeneration with respect to that which is the spirituality of us, the Westerners.

Above all since the world war (and this confirms once again its unwholesome and negative root), the forms of such a spiritualism have had an impressive development. There are the thousands and thousands of sects preaching the doctrine of the super-man in the women's organizations and those of the *lesser-men* of the protestant lands. There is the unwholesome interest in the problems of the subconscious, of mediumism, of the meta-psychic. There is the way of the "returns" to old religious forms. There is, finally, a mysticism that is more or less pantheistic, vague, proselytizing, sensualist, humanist, vegetarian. However great the variety of all these forms may be, they all fall under one and the same meaning, which reflects only a sense of evasion, avoidance, fatigue. It is the soul of the West that vacillates, becomes dislocated and anemic. The eye no longer sees it exist except in the closed and blind world down below: behind the cold and lucid lords of the algebras dragging the forces of matter, in the gold that dictates the law to the governors and the governed, in the machines where, day after day heroisms deprived of light are launched through the sky and the oceans.

The lack of all drive in favor of the liberation of this plan of values, living within this plan, with a view to their reaffirmation and integration into a higher order of an anti-mystical spirituality, is the true limit of the modern world, its agent of crystallization and of decadence. The occidental tradition will not be revived except when a new culture, which is not spellbound by the hallucination of material reality and of human psychology, shall create healthy attitudes of science of absolute action and individuality, beyond the mist of "spiritualism."

And understanding nothing else but that by the word *magic,* we say: it is by means of a *magical era* that the West will be able to leave the *dark era* and the era of iron. No *return,* no alteration. In an era of active realism, transcendent and intensely individual, our occidental tradition will stand up again on its own root, which has no contact with the asceticism and universalizing contemplativity of the past. We shall thus find the Light that descended from the North to the South (the artico-atlantic spirit) and passed from the West to the East, leaving everywhere the same traces of a cosmic symbolism and of words in which resonates the "great voice of things," as well as of a blood that is heroic, active, conquering. This era, which will give back to the world the law of a clear vision and a precise action even in the spiritual world, takes up again, while guarding itself from all romanticism and from all "utopia," the virile word of "will to advancement," which excludes all nostalgia, all weakness of aspirations to nirvana.

53

THE MAGIC OF CREATION

Julius Evola wrote this piece for La Flèche *No. 3, December 15, 1930. Relations between Evola and Naglowska continued to be good, as shown by his articles for* La Flèche *and his translating of* Magia Sexualis, *which Naglowska published in November, 1931, and for which Evola also wrote a foreword. This article was signed "Jules Evola."*

Fortified and brought back to life by the sacred power of rite, Man participates in the Supreme Virtue: he becomes a creator.

But know: for us *create* is not the pale metaphor of which mortals speak. For us, to create means to give life to distinct and real beings by a direct act of thought that gives soul to a fluidic form objectivized outside of our own matter.

You will understand this mystery when you cease to know only the dead thought that projects inert shadows of verbal concepts and abstractions and is lost in polemics and sterile ideals.

You will understand this mystery when you know deep thought, that which rises from your whole body like a heavy and vibrant thing, plastic and *elemental*. It is the breath of the flesh and bones, the desire of the stone.

Scorn illusory idealisms, jealous guardians of the principle of incorporeality of thought. Recognize the latter as a concrete and living thing, as a reality in space and even if freed from certain laws of nature.

You will know then that concentration is not the cerebral effort that is content to send back all images in order to remain immobile, but the creation of a current, of an energetic fluid, of a vibration that assumes a unique direction in giving a form, a rhythm, to the mass of the thought-force that you feel rush up from the depths of the body.

You fix some images in the internal light, and these images become for you like skeletons that your thought-force fills with vibrant substance as it gives them the fire of the soul.

Then an entity is created that can be bound to an object.

It is thus that magicians bind to amulets a "center of influence" oriented according to a specific chosen quality. That can be the determined will to accomplish this or that act, it can be a feeling, an emotion, a passion; it matters little.

Upon contact with the object, thus saturated by a long and profound concentration, anyone immediately feels the effect and experiences, according to the case, love, hate, anguish, or ecstasy.

The work of creation thus understood can also be accomplished by a collectivity, provided that the currents that emanate from it spontaneously or by virtue of a rite have the same direction and an identical vibration and intention. It must be as a single and unique thought on the part of all the members of the collectivity.

In the Indies they tell of a beggar who was asked by his mother, a woman of exceptional religious faith, to bring back to her a relic from the holy place to which he was going. Not having found the relic, but also not wanting to disappoint his mother, the beggar brought back to her a tooth taken from the jaw of a dog's corpse. He told her that this tooth had belonged to a famous boddhisattva.

The old woman believed him and the legend of the holy relic brought back by the mendicant soon spread through the country. From all parts, the faithful came to adore the so-called relic. But here is what was surprising: quite soon afterward, the tooth from the dead dog actually took on marvelous powers. Indeed, one saw strange glows separate themselves from this poor little thing.

So, it is the concentration of spirit of these beings animated by faith that really deposited and created in the dead dog's tooth these virtues that it had not had before.

More or less the same phenomenon is found in the great and sometimes formidable psychic currents, which even act through whole generations, starting from a symbolic object: a cross, a flag, a rod.

It is not a vain superstition that has pushed men from the earliest centuries to venerate certain objects, tombs, sanctuaries. These things, adored by the peoples, truly have a special power: they exalt, give enthusiasm, animate, and fortify by virtue of the mechanism that we have just explained.

When one comes to the point of totally possessing such power of concentration as we have described, one can also be a creator spontaneously and without knowing it. For example it can happen that, while one is deeply absorbed by a given thought, the latter may take the form of an apparition visible to persons who are sensitive to this effect. That is the cause of certain mediumistic phantoms that suddenly place themselves beside you, sometimes without you even perceiving them right away.

Bringing this power to its supreme degree, one can come to create a divine being and make it live, suffer, and love in a person chosen for this purpose.

That is the mystery of spiritual paternity or maternity. It is impenetrable for whoever is not there yet, but . . . everything is a mystery for him who does not *know*.

NOTES

INTRODUCTION: THE ORGAN OF MAGICAL ACTION

1. Schreck, and Schreck, *Demons of the Flesh,* 278.

2. Pluquet, *La Sophiale,* 7.

3. Deveney and Rosemont, *Paschal Beverly Randolph: A Nineteenth-Century Black American Spiritualist,* XVIII.

4. Ibid.

5. Alexandrian, *Les libérateurs de l'amour,* 185–206.

6. Naglowska, "Mon chef spirituel," *La Flèche, Organe d'Action Magique* 10 (February 15, 1932) 2–3.

7. Evola, *The Metaphysics of Sex,* 261.

8. Randolph, *Magia Sexualis,* French translation by Maria de Naglowska An English translation was published by Inner Traditions in 2012 as part of this series.

9. Pluquet, *La Sophiale* 8, 14.

10. Naglowska, *Le Rite sacré de l'amour magique* (Supplément de *La Flèche Organe d'Action Magique,* Paris: 1932). An English translation titled *The Sacred Rite of Magical Love* was published by Inner Traditions in 2012 as part of this series.

11. Naglowska, *La Lumière du sexe.* An English translation titled *The Light of Sex* was published by Inner Traditions in 2011 as part of this series.

12. Naglowska, *Le Mystère de la pendaison.* An English translation titled *Advanced Sex Magic* was published by Inner Traditions in 2011 as part of this series.

13. Pluquet, *La Sophiale,* 12.
14. Naglowska, "Avant la Guerre de 1936," *La Flèche Organe d'Action Magique* 20 (15 January 1935): 3.
15. Pluquet, *La Sophiale,* 14.
16. Ibid., 13–14.
17. Ibid., 12.

CHAPTER 10. THE COMMANDMENTS OF THE THIRD TERM OF THE TRINITY

1. Naglowska, *The Light of Sex: Initiation, Magic, and Sacrament,* 32–33.

CHAPTER 21. THE MAGIC SQUARE

1. René Thimmy (Maurice Magre), *La magie à Paris,* 74–79.

CHAPTER 43. "THE SPIRITUAL TREASON OF FREEMASONRY" COMMITTED BY J. MARQUÈS-RIVIÈRE

1. Marquès-Rivière, *La trahison spirituelle de la franc-maçonnerie.*

CHAPTER 46. THE "POLAIRES"

1. Bhotiva, *Asia Mysteriosa,* 5–41.

BIBLIOGRAPHY

Alexandrian, Sarane. *Les libérateurs de l'amour.* Paris: Éditions du Seuil, 1977.

Anel-Kham, B. (pseudonym of Henri Meslin). *Théorie et pratique de la magie sexuelle.* Paris: Librairie Astra, 1938.

Bardon, Franz. *Initiation into Hermetics.* Salt Lake City: Merkur Publishing, 2005.

Bhotiva, Zam. *Asia mysteriosa et le mystère des polaires.* Combronde: Éditions de Janvier, 1995.

Deveney, John Patrick, and Franklin Rosemont. *Paschal Beverly Randolph: A Nineteenth-Century Black American Spiritualist.* Albany: SUNY Press, 1997.

Evola, Julius. *The Metaphysics of Sex.* New York: Inner Traditions International, 1983. Reprinted as *Eros and the Mysteries of Love.* Rochester, Vt.: Inner Traditions International, 1991.

Garçon, Maurice. *Vintras, hérésiarque et prophète.* Paris: Librairie Critique Émile Nourry, 1928.

Gengenbach, Ernest de. *L'Expérience démoniaque.* Paris: Eric Losfeld, 1968.

Geyraud, Pierre (pseudonym of l'Abbé Pierre Guyader). Paris: Éditions Émile-Paul Frères, 1937.

Godwin, Joscelyn, Christian Chanel, and John P. Deveney. *The Hermetic Brotherhood of Luxor.* York Beach, Maine: Samuel Weiser, Inc., 1995.

Hakl, Hans Thomas. "Maria de Naglowska and the Confrérie de la Flèche d'Or." *Politica Hermetica* 20 (2006): 113–23.

Levi, Eliphas (Alphonse Louis Constant). *The Book of Splendours.* York Beach, Maine: Samuel Weiser, Inc., 1984.

Marquès-Rivière, Jean. *La Trahison de la F:.M:..* Paris: Éditions des Portiques, 1931.

Naglowska, Maria de. *La paix et son principal obstacle.* Geneva: N.p., 1918.

———. *La Lumière du sexe.* Paris: Éditions de la Flèche, 1932.

———. *Le Rite sacré de l'amour magique: Aveu 26.1.* Paris: Supplément de "La Flèche" Organe d'Action Magique, 1932.

———. *Le Mystère de la pendaison.* Paris: Éditions de la Flèche, 1934.

———. *La Flèche, Organe d'Action Magique* 1–20 (Oct. 15, 1930–Jan. 15, 1935).

———. *Advanced Sex Magic: The Hanging Mystery Initiation.* Translated by Donald Traxler. Rochester, Vt.: Inner Traditions, 2011.

———. *The Light of Sex: Initiation, Magic, and Sacrament.* Translated by Donald Traxler. Rochester, Vt.: Inner Traditions, 2011.

———. *The Sacred Rite of Magical Love: A Ceremony of Word and Flesh.* Translated by Donald Traxler. Rochester, Vt.: Inner Traditions, 2012.

Pluquet, Marc. *La Sophiale: Maria de Naglowska, sa vie—son oeuvre.* Montpeyroux: Éditions Gouttelettes de Rosée, n.d.

Randolph, Paschal Beverly. Compiled and translated by Maria de Naglowska. *Magia Sexualis.* Paris: Robert Télin. 1931.

———. *Magia Sexualis: Sexual Practices for Magical Power.* Translated by Donald Traxler. Rochester, Vt.: Inner Traditions, 2012.

Schreck, Nikolas, and Zeena. *Demons of the Flesh.* Clerkenwell: Creation Books, 2002.

Simanovitch, Aron. *Raspoutine.* Translated by S. de Leo and Maria de Naglowska. Paris: Librairie Gallimard for NRF, 1930.

Thimmy, René. *La Magie à Paris.* Paris: Les Éditions de France, 1934.

Vintras, Eugène. *L'Évangile Éternel.* London: Trubner & Co., 1857. (Nabu Reprint, 2010; PDF also available from archive.org.)

INDEX

BOOKS OF RELATED INTEREST

The Light of Sex
Initiation, Magic, and Sacrament
by Maria de Naglowska

Advanced Sex Magic
The Hanging Mystery Initiation
by Maria de Naglowska

The Sacred Rite of Magical Love
A Ceremony of Word and Flesh
by Maria de Naglowska

Magia Sexualis
Sexual Practices for Magical Power
by Paschal Beverly Randolph and Maria de Naglowska

Carnal Alchemy
Sado-Magical Techniques for Pleasure, Pain, and Self-Transformation
by Stephen E. Flowers, Ph.D., and Crystal Dawn Flowers

Lords of the Left-Hand Path
Forbidden Practices and Spiritual Heresies
by Stephen E. Flowers, Ph.D.

Introduction to Magic
Rituals and Practical Techniques for the Magus
by Julius Evola and the UR Group

The Secret History of Western Sexual Mysticism
Sacred Practices and Spiritual Marriage
by Arthur Versluis

INNER TRADITIONS • BEAR & COMPANY
P.O. Box 388
Rochester, VT 05767
1-800-246-8648
www.InnerTraditions.com

Or contact your local bookseller